PSYCHOANALYTIC STUDIES OF RELIGION

Recent Titles in
Bibliographies and Indexes in Religious Studies

Judaism and Human Rights in Contemporary Thought:
A Bibliographical Survey
S. Daniel Breslauer

Religion in Postwar China: A Critical Analysis and Annotated Bibliography
David C. Yu, compiler

Islam in China: A Critical Bibliography
Raphael Israeli, with the assistance of Lyn Gorman

Jonathan Edwards: An Annotated Bibliography, 1979–1993
M. X. Lesser, compiler

Religion and the American Experience, The Twentieth Century:
A Bibliography of Doctoral Dissertations
Arthur P. Young and E. Jens Holley, compilers

Religious Education, 1960–1993: An Annotated Bibliography
D. Campbell Wyckoff and George Brown, Jr., compilers

South Asian Religions in the Americas: An Annotated Bibliography
of Immigrant Religious Traditions
John Y. Fenton

Micronesian Religion and Lore: A Guide to Sources, 1525–1990
Douglas Haynes and William L. Wuerch

Christian Voluntarism in Britain and North America:
A Bibliography and Critical Assessment
William H. Brackney

Ecology, Justice, and Christian Faith: A Critical Guide to the Literature
Peter W. Bakken, Joan Gibb Engel, and J. Ronald Engel

Modern American Popular Religion: A Critical Assessment and
Annotated Bibliography
Charles H. Lippy

Reincarnation: A Selected Annotated Bibliography
Lynn Kear

PSYCHOANALYTIC STUDIES OF RELIGION

A Critical Assessment and
Annotated Bibliography

Benjamin Beit-Hallahmi

Bibliographies and Indexes in Religious Studies,
Number 39
G. E. Gorman, Advisory Editor

GREENWOOD PRESS
Westport, Connecticut • London

Library of Congress Cataloging-in-Publication Data

Beit-Hallahmi, Benjamin.
   Psychoanalytic studies of religion : a critical assessment and
annotated bibliography / Benjamin Beit-Hallahmi.
      p.   cm.—(Bibliographies and indexes in religious studies,
   ISSN 0742-6836 ; no. 39)
   Includes indexes.
   ISBN 0-313-27362-6 (alk. paper)
   1. Psychoanalysis and religion—Bibliography.   I. Title.
II. Series.
Z7204.P8B44   1996
[BF175]
016.2'001'9—dc20   96-18524

British Library Cataloguing in Publication Data is available.

Library of Congress Catalog Card Number: 96-18524
ISBN: 0-313-27362-6
ISSN: 0742-6836

First published in 1996

Greenwood Press, 88 Post Road West, Westport, CT 06881
An imprint of Greenwood Publishing Group, Inc.

Printed in the United States of America

The paper used in this book complies with the
Permanent Paper Standard issued by the National
Information Standards Organization (Z39.48–1984).

10 9 8 7 6 5 4 3 2

CONTENTS

SERIES FOREWORD

We could say much the same thing for the psychology of religion as a whole: too naturalistic and scientific for the religious, too religious for the psychologists. Yet for the psychology of religion the outcome is not popularity. Although a surprisingly large proportion of the world's most eminent psychologists have made significant contributions to it, the psychology of religion is often neglected, if not treated with condescension or contempt.

-- David M. Wulff *Psychology of Religion*

[Freud] underwent a long and intense introspective period, characterized by tension between a religious ethos and the secular, modern ethos. This tension was resolved by the creation of an utterly new system of ideas which were neither religious in any traditional or conventional sense nor scientific in the sense of the exact science of nineteenth century physics and chemistry, but which were, as we are accustomed to say today, psychological in nature.

-- Peter Homans, "A Personal Struggle with Religion"

The psychoanalytic study of religion and its parent discipline, the psychology of religion, evoke a broad spectrum of responses from both scholars and the general public. Social scientists, for example, sometimes dismiss the psychology of religion as being unscientific; equally, many religious professionals discount the findings of psychology and psychoanalysis as anti religious. As one wag has said, psychology is nothing more than a psycho-phantasmagoris pseudo-science that seeks to tell us what we already know intuitively in language that we do not understand. Add to this popular perception of psychology the conservative religious view that psychology and psychoanalysis are destructive of belief and faith, and one sees that the psychology of religion has enjoyed a rather negative reputation in many circles. In our view such dichotomous reactions to both the psychology and the psychoanalytic study of religion go back to the very origins of these complementary disciplines, as a bridge between what Homans terms a "religious ethos" and a "secular, modern ethos." True, sometimes repudiation of religion results from the psychoanalytic study of it, but equally often there is an assimilation of ideas from both psychology and religion in which one informs the other. "From my studies of the lives of the first psychologists, I am inclined to arrive at the conclusion that these psychologies not only repudiate the Western religious tradition...; they also derive something very important from the Western religious tradition. This something is, in short, their moral code, a residue of morality"(1). It is this bridging feature that in our view makes the psychoanalytic study not only fascinating but also essential for a modern understanding of religious belief and action.

Many maintain that the critique of religion that characterizes the psychoanalytic study of religion does little more than reduce religious impulses to neuroses or infantile tendencies. This may well be the case with those who adhere to the classic Freudian view that religious beliefs are grounded in childhood wishes and fears. "The irrationality of religion's motives and the repression that keeps hidden its all-too-human origins are signaled, Freud argued, by the air of inviolable sanctity that surrounds religious ideas and the compulsive qualities of sacred rites reminiscent of neurotic 'ritual'"(2). The techniques and insights for psychoanalysis do not always lead one down this path, however. Jung, for example, found religion to be an essential part of the human psyche, and he utilized religion as one tool in understanding this psyche. One might argue, as Homans does, that Jung's development of the school of analytical psychology incorporates in it his personal rejection of religion; others, however, emphasize how Jung's analytical psychology provides "...a truly penetrating understanding of the religious life, without reducing it through causal explanation"(3).

Even those who feel that there is benefit to be derived from the psychological or psychoanalytic study of religion admit that flaws and shortcomings are all too dominant. As Benjamin Beit-Hallahmi states later in this work, "one of the common complaints is the psychoanalytic tendency to over-interpret and over-psychologize, while neglecting the historical and cultural components of the phenomena under analysis." This may be termed psychological imperialism. At the same time, there is a kind of scientific imperialism that sees psychological and psychoanalytic understanding as definitely of a second or third order because it does not adhere to the "pure" scientific method in the sense that classical physics or chemistry do (as suggested above by Homans).

The reality is that the psychoanalytic study of religion has contributed significantly to our understanding of religion as both an institution and as a field of academic endeavor. Psychoanalytic understanding has helped us unravel the complex relationships between culture and religion, and between individual belief and social and cultural needs. In a sense the psychoanalytic study of religion is a process that enables us to grasp the meaning of religious belief and practice for individuals and, through them, for their communities of faith. The assumption is that religious acts are always psychologically meaningful and that religious beliefs and behavior can be analyzed in order to discover an unconscious meaning. As Beit-Hallahmi maintains, "psychoanalysis is the only major psychological theory which offers an explanation of religion as part of a comprehensive theory of human behavior, in which religion is presented as an instance of general psychological forces in action." The psychoanlytic study of religion draws upon the theory and praxis of many other disciplines, including psychology and religion, and also anthropology, medicine, history, sociology, education and theology. It is, in an academic sense, a complex field of study forming a bridge across the sciences, social sciences and humanities. This emerges with clarity in the essay, "Psychoanalytic Studies of Religion: A Critical Assessment," that opens the present volume. Here the key references spread across psychoanalysis and psychology, religion and theology to sociology, anthropology, and many other disciplines. Thus from an academic viewpoint the psychoanalytic study of religion draws on a wide range of cognate disciplines, which gives its literature an unusual breadth. Furthermore, within itself this multifaceted discipline manifests a complex network of theoretical frameworks that are not easily traced through the literature.

Many of us, whether students or scholars, are not fully aware of the complex disciplinary origins of the psychoanalytic study of religion. Furthermore, the substantial corpus of literature devoted to this field will surprise all but the most accomplished scholars and practitioners. For these combined reasons it was deemed appropriate that we commission a critical guide to the essential literature on psychoanalytic approaches to religion in this biographical series. To assume the responsibility of compiling such a bibliography we have been able to draw upon the expertise of a well-established scholar of the psychology of religion, Dr. Benjamin Beit-Hallahmi, Professor of Psychology at the University of Haifa. Dr. Beit-Hallahmi is perhaps best known for his 1989 publication, *Prolegomena to the Psychological Study of Religion,* and the more recent *Illustrated Encyclopedia of Active New Religions, Sects and Cults* (1992); he has also contributed some eighty papers on psychoanalysis and religion, and on political affairs in the modern Middle East, to journals in North America, Europe and elsewhere. These wide-ranging interests and scholarly pursuits make him well-suited to the task of working on such an eclectic, catholic topic as psychoanalysis and religion. In addition, Dr. Beit-Hallahmi is no stranger to the painstaking attention to detail required when undertaking bibliographical work, having first entered this arena nearly twenty years ago with *Psychoanalysis and Religion: A Bibliography* (1978).

In *Psychoanalytic Studies of Religion: A Critical Assessment and Annotated Bibliography,* Dr. Beit-Hallahmi accomplished two important tasks. In Part 1 ("Psychoanalytic Studies of Religion: A Critical Assessment") he presents an introductory bibliographical essay on key aspects of psychoanalysis and religion: the theory of psychoanalysis, its historical development, the place of Freud, types of analysis and critiques. This discussion contains numerous references to items in the bibliography, thereby leading readers from general discussion to specific entries. Part 2, then, is the detailed bibliography on the psychoanalytic study of religion, consisting of twenty-one topical sections (Ritual, Conversion, Judaism, etc.) in which Dr. Beit-Hallahmi annotates more than 600 items that he believes represent the most important literature on the subject (in his words, "the essential literature reflecting and expressing psychoanalytic approaches to religion".) His annotations are brief but precise, indicating the content and value of individual entries.

In this volume Dr. Beit-Hallahmi presents a record of the scholarship on psychoanalysis and religion and offers a summary of the key literature as an aid to further study. In both regards he has more than met our expectations, providing a volume that offers at once a clear overview of the field and a detailed guide to appropriate published resources. In fulfilling these interrelated tasks he provides scholars and practitioners in psychology, psychoanalysis, counselling and religion with a valuable compendium that will serve as a major resource well into the future. Beyond doubt the ideas and themes discussed here will continue to evolve, and this volume will serve as a biographical benchmark in this evolution. At the end of the day we can but concur with the author's own conclusion:

> After reviewing this large body of literature, we should have the right to ask whether it has really taught us something we did not know before, something we could not have otherwise known. The answer is clearly in the affirmative. Psychoanalysis has clearly led to a revolution in the study of religion in general and in the psychology of religion in particular. It has taught us many things we did not know.

Therefore, we are pleased to include this publication in Bibliographies and Indexes in Religious Studies, and we commend it as another valuable addition to the series.

NOTES

1. Peter Homans, "A personal Struggle with Religions: Significant Facts in the Lives and Work of the First Psychologists." *The Journal of Religion* 62 (1982): 141-142.

2. David M. Wulff, *Psychology of Religion: Classic and Contemporary Views* (New York: John Wiley and Sons, 1991), p. 17.

3. *Ibid.*, p. 18.

Dr. G.E. Gorman
Advisory Editor
Charles Sturt University - Riverina
July 1995

ACKNOWLEDGMENTS

My interest in the psychoanalytic study of religion has been nurtured and supported by many friends and by the various institutions with which I have been affiliated since the 1970s. Among the many friends and colleagues I would like to mention by name are Daniel Friedmann, Nicole Lapierre, Arthur Dole, Jerome Weiman, Madeleine Tress, Yoram Bilu, Mimi Halkin, Peter Homans, Wayne Proudfoot, Harriet Lutzky, Eliezer Witztum and Angela Greenson. Among the institutions let me mention the Centre d'Etudes Transdisciplinaires of CNRS in Paris, which enabled me to bring this work to fruition, the Graduate School of Education at the University of Pennsylvania, the Department of Psychology at Michigan State University, the Department of Religion at Columbia University, the Department of Psychology at the University of Haifa, the Library of the University of Haifa, and the Research Authority at the University of Haifa. I owe a special debt to the Rev. G. E. Gorman, who first asked me to prepare this volume, and who has been patient and helpful in his role as series editor. The responsibility for misjudgments, errors, and omissions is mine only.

INTRODUCTION

The aim of this volume is to offer the first critical guide to the essential literature reflecting and expressing psychoanalytic approaches to religion. Existing reference works provide good bibliographical listings, but do not give the reader critical annotations and evaluations. The emphasis here is on *critical* assessments, steering the user towards works of lasting value, and away from the trivial and the useless. There is necessarily a judgmental, if not "subjective", element in this work, which is by definition a selective introduction to the field. Every introductory survey of this kind has to be selective, but its author needs to make clear, as much as possible, its guiding principles, or biases. Not everything deserves to be mentioned, and the boundaries of our domain need to be determined. Our first priority has been to include publications clearly aimed at continuing the Freudian tradition and contributing to the psychoanalytic psychology of religion. A second priority has been accorded critical discussions of specific works or of the whole approach.

The literature covered consists of psychoanalytic publications which have seen the light of day between 1920 and 1993. The language is English, which has been the *lingua franca* of psychoanalysis since the 1920s, and was used by Freud himself. This book covers the literature written in response to Freud, but not Freud's own writings. Assessing Freud's work is beyond our scope here, and it is limited to post-Freudian writings.

CRITERIA FOR INCLUSION

Together with defining the boundaries of psychoanalysis (see below), the first boundary to be marked is that of content. How do we define religion, and what topics tangential to religion can be included? Religion is defined here as a belief system which includes, and is usually based on, the notion of a "supernatural", invisible world, inhabited by souls, divine beings, and other "psychic" entities (Cf. 302: Numbered references refer to items in the Annotated Bibliography). Works dealing with folklore and folk superstition as their main topics have been excluded.

The field covered is that of psychoanalytic contributions to the psychology of religion. We are trying to include every coherent attempt, guided by psychoanalytic theory, to offer an explanation, an understanding, an interpretation of religion or religious behavior. In addition, important critical discussions and overviews of the psychoanalytic approach were included.

How does one decide whether a given contribution is indeed psychoanalytic? In most cases there is a telltale vocabulary and familiar terminology (primary process, projection,

xiv Psychoanalytic Studies of Religion

compulsive neurosis, object relations, identification, identity, dream process, regression in the service of the ego"). In other cases, we find some authors who present their intellectual genealogy which starts with Freud, or it can be inferred from citations or citation sequences from Freud on. Often there are no citations outside the classical canon, as authors are all too eager to make clear their allegiance. Some authors are all too anxious to proclaim their theoretical loyalty, and engage in ancestor worship, trying to prove that their own contribution was anticipated by Freud, thus obviating any need for it.

Sources in which contributions are published may serve as another easy guideline. We can easily make up a list of more-or-less "orthodox" psychoanalytic journals, and in effect most of the literature covered here comes from these. Only publications where religion is the main topic were selected, in most cases, and we have not included publications where religion is mentioned in passing (with a few rare and deserving exceptions). The latter number in the thousands and are also of value, but are simply beyond the scope of this work. As mentioned above, contributions critical of the psychoanalytic approach have also been included when judged to be of lasting worth.

CRITERIA FOR EXCLUSION

The bibliographic screening process started with checking the existing listings in the field. A closer scrutiny has shown that numerous items listed in various bibliographies as related to religion and psychoanalysis are actually irrelevant. Some are classified because of title alone, not content. What we are covering here is not "depth psychology", but psychoanalysis. Not every writer suggesting a link between sexual motives and religion should be included. Not every author discussing "unconscious" elements in religion is following Freud's ideas.

Not included in this work are contributions to either religious apologetics or pastoral counseling (cf. 101). The literature of religious apologetics includes attempts to defend religion or defend religious structures as true, useful, and worthy of defense and support. This literature aims to be useful to religion in general, to religious organizations, or to the clergy, and represents a branch of theology, guided by a strong commitment to religion. It does not necessarily contribute to the analysis of religion, but seeks to defend or strengthen it. One sure sign of an apologetic intent is the phrasing of one's topic as psychoanalysis *and* religion, rather than as a project in the psychoanalytic interpretation *of* religion. This voluminous literature can teach us much about the state of religious faith among certain intellectuals, theologians, and church leaders, but it has few insights to offer us about religion from a psychoanalytic viewpoint. Despite the fact that the literature of apologetics represents much in the way of intellectual effort, it leads to little in the way of psychoanalytic understanding. A few apologetic articles are included in the book only because they have special historical significance, some influence (reflected in citations), and have also contributed to the psychological analysis of religion.

To summarize, the guidelines in developing this annotated bibliography have been selectivity and significance. This book is intended to be a working tool, and its intended audience is scholars and students in the fields of psychoanalysis, psychology, sociology, anthropology, history, literature, folklore, and religion.

Part 1 of this book is an introduction to, and a brief critical assessment of, the psychoanalytic literature covered in Part 2. It attempts a general definition of psychoanalytic theories, surveys their historical development, and then goes on to look critically at the attempt, now three generations old, to solve the riddle of religion through psychodynamic insights. Part 2 contains the annotated entries, divided into twenty-one topics. The aim of the annotations is to give the reader a summary of the entry, as well as an evaluation of its content.

Part 1

PSYCHOANALYTIC STUDIES OF RELIGION: A CRITICAL ASSESSMENT

*

THE BASIC THEORY

What is psychoanalytic theory? We can recognize it either through its vocabulary (to some, its "jargon") or through its bibliographic ancestry, its references. Psychoanalytic writings can be recognized through their use of a common vocabulary which has become, over the years, part of everyday intellectual discourse: conscious and unconscious, id, ego, superego, neuroses, anxiety, and defense mechanisms. If one cites Freud, Jones, and Erikson in writing about religion, chances are this publication will be identified as psychoanalytic. Publication source is another criterion. If an article has been published in the *Psychoanalytic Review* or the *International Journal of Psycho-Analysis*, we know with certainty that it conforms to the psychoanalytic frame of reference.

This is a large body of literature, created by many authors who share common assumptions about personality dynamics. Psychoanalysis is known today as a personality theory, as a theory (and a practice) of psychotherapy, and then as a psychology of culture. Here we are going to deal with psychoanalysis as a general theory of human behavior, leading to applications either in psychotherapy or in the analysis of culture. We are interested in the treatment of religion as one variant by it. The structural point of view states that all behavior has structural determinants. The latter states that all behavior is part of a sequence, and the present form of the personality was created by its antecedents. The adaptive point of view states that all behavior is determined by reality.

Two assumptions were suggested by Freud himself (1915/1916) to characterize his approach. The first states that all psychic processes are strictly determined (no accidents, chance events, or miracles), the second that unconscious mental processes exist, and exert significant influences on behavior. These unconscious forces shape much of the individual's emotional and interpersonal experiences.

The Role of the Unconscious

We all are ready to admit momentary, fleeting, childish, irrational thoughts, as in hypnagogic experiences. These experiences are marginal. Psychoanalysis claims that they may be more than that, and that unconscious processes are possibly the main determinants of observable behavior. The emphasis on the unconscious part of the personality can be summed up as follows: part of the personality is unconscious, and it is the more important part; the unconscious is the repository of significant early experience; in the adult, unconscious ideas are projected, creating severe distortions of reality, especially interpersonal reality.

Primary process, which rules the deeper, unconscious, layers of the personality, obeys the pleasure principle, which aims at achieving a hallucinated reality of the desired object. The secondary process obeys the reality principle, and involves the postponement of immediate gratification and the testing of imaginary ideas against the real world.

Motivation

Psychoanalysis is a theory of struggle, conflict, and compromise, assuming the dynamic nature of human behavior, which always results from conflict and change. Additional assumptions deal with overdetermination and the multiple functions of behavior. The overdetermination assumption states that any segment of behavior may have many preceding causes. This is tied to a developmental, or historical emphasis, leading us to seek first causes in any individual's personal history and unique experiences. The psychoanalytic view of human motivation is often regarded as utterly pessimistic. Judging by their conscious and unconscious drives, humans may become nasty and brutish, aggressive, infantile, libido driven. However, beyond this bleak picture of immorality and even perversity lies the capacity for sublimation, love and culture.

Personality Development

Freud's ideas about development focus on what has come to be called psychosexual development. That is the transformation, molding, and sometimes perversion, of biologically determined erotic drives in early childhood. Its focal point is the Oedipus complex, woven around the child's attachment to its parents as love objects or identification models between the ages of three and six. Early childhood experiences serve as historical precedents in every individual's life, and in the life of every human culture. The reconstruction of personality development is based on the infant's and child's way of thinking, which is impossible to recover. It is based on behavioral observations and sometimes inferred, like unconscious processes.

The never-ending impact of childhood is a central issue defining psychoanalysis. The infant's irrational wish fulfillment is supposed to be left behind by the adult, but childhood is always alive behind the facade of adulthood. The legacy of childhood is far from marginal and is co-existent with the adult level of thinking and functioning. We can observe it on both the individual and the cultural levels.

Structure and Function

The psychoanalytic view of personality structure can be characterized as a translation of the conflict idea into presumed struggling entities. It is an internal war of all against all, as the id relentlessly fights the superego, and the ego has to cope with both. It is this permanent structural conflict which leads to neurosis (or worse), as the ego is sometimes incapable of satisfying the warring sides without paying a heavy toll in adaptation.

Defense Mechanisms and the Distortion of Reality

Psychoanalysis in its rationalistic view of individuals and culture is a theory of reality distortion. Different stages in theory offer differing ideas of how we distort and what kinds of projection we follow. The psychoanalytic view of maladaptive behavior emphasizes its continuity with adaptive behavior and leads to viewing pathology as a useful analogy of cultural structures. Moreover, maladaptive behavior is analyzed through the detailed recognition of defensive sequences. Not only the final outcome — symptoms — but the internal sequence leading to it are carefully outlined. There is an ideal of flexibility and moderation, as opposed to ⅃igidity which is pathological, but inevitable. Rigidity in the form of rituals and ritualized defenses become one of the sources of analogies for religion. The analytic starting point of symptom, syndrome and the search for their unconscious background served as the model for examining religion.

Universality

Psychoanalysis assumes the psychic unity of mankind, which is significant when we deal with cultural traditions. In terms of the basic theory, going back to Freud's *Interpretation of Dreams*, universality is found at the most basic level of body, birth, sex, and death. Psychoanalytic approaches of all theoretical stripes (classical, ego-psychological, and object relations) claim universal, transcultural, and ahistorical validity. This assumed universality of psychoanalysis is definitely tied to a universalistic, humanistic assumption of human brotherhood.

This working assumption does have a particular relevance to the phenomenon of religion. Universal themes in religious mythology are the result and reflection of the psychic unity of humankind, which in turn is the consequence of common psychological structures and common early experiences shared by all humankind. The same basic psychological processes and complexes are expressed in individual products (dreams, stories, and daydreams), and in cultural products (art, literature, folklore, wit, religion, law, and science), because these complexes are basic and central to human experience. A phenomenon like castration anxiety, which is basic and universal, is going to be reflected in numerous individual and cultural products.

The Governing Metaphor

What unites most strands of psychoanalytic theory is the governing metaphor of conflict. Beyond visible conflicts invisible ones are found, even if it is hard to locate them.
This is inevitable in relations among humans. The family, locus of love and devotion, is actually a battlefield, but it only reflects the wider reality of both individual souls and human society as a whole. This is the source of what has to be called the tragic dimension in psychoanalytic literature, a deep recognition of human limitations and a realistic approach to one's chances of achieving happiness, which is clearly secular and humanistic.

HISTORICAL DEVELOPMENT OF THE PSYCHOANALYTIC APPROACH

Because psychoanalysis was created in the context of the medical practice of one clinical neurologist, seeking to cure those defined as neurotic, its historical goal since 1895 has been that of uncovering the meaning and motivations of symptoms. Subsequently, covering the unconscious meaning of behavior has taken on wider dimensions, including the cultural. The historical starting point in clinical work has always been reflected in writings on religion. "Classical" Theory, as contained in Freud's writings, is not strictly a formal, theoretical, system. We can speak of a theoretical melange, an untidy, metaphorical collection of ideas, brilliant observations, or travel notes, of a psychological anthropologist.

Freud's theory kept developing and changing — we can speak of the theory in 1895 as Theory A, in 1900-1915 as Theory B, and in 1920-1930 as Theory C, with clear differences among the three. The body of classical Freudian theory is defined by the texts of *The Interpretation of Dreams* (1900) and *The Psychopathology of Everyday Life* (1901).

These classical texts containing the heart of Freud's early formulations are recapitulated more systematically in the *Introductory Lectures* (1915/1916).

There are several possible levels of writing the history of psychoanalysis. There is the level of theory, dealing with personality structure and its versions. There is the clinical level, with the movement in concepts from hysteria, to neurosis, to personality disorders, to schizoid and borderline states in today's parlance. The notion of a borderline personality, characterized by a deficient sense of reality and self-identity, depression, narcissism, and inappropriate behavior appeared in the 1960s. Its popularity was later shadowed by the concept of the narcissistic personality. It is clear that the same individual will have been diagnosed differently in different periods. These changes could be judged to be progressive developments and increases in competence, or just fads and fashions.

The Three Stages of Psychoanalysis

We can speak of three historical stages, tied to clinical problems, of id psychology, ego psychology, and superego psychology. In the first stage, the phenomena dealt with were hysteria and related symptoms, viewed as related to the effects of id impulses. In later stages, specific symptoms were ignored as character problems came to the fore. Later on personality, or character, disorders were dropped and the problem was defined as distorted relations, tied to distorted perceptions of reality in general.

Ego Psychology

The first major change was in moving away from instincts to adaptation and defense, i.e. adaptation to the environment and the defense of the ego from internal anxiety and external dangers. Ego psychology means an emphasis on adaptation to reality, through unconscious defense mechanisms as well as realistic actions. Ego psychology emphasizes the understanding of defenses and the motives for defense (see A. Freud, 1946). Psychoanalytic ego psychology has suggested that there is a natural limit to rational reality testing, and the tension of rationality is relieved by opportunities for regression in the service of the ego. Other ego defense mechanisms, which play a major role in religious behavior, include sublimation, identification, projection, displacement and reaction-formation.

The development of ego-psychology has affected much psychoanalytic work on religion (see 723). In addition to unconscious defense mechanisms, there are also ego functions such as sense perception, memory, language, judgment, reality testing, suspending the last one to achieve regression in service of ego. This relatively new concept intends to remind us that not every regression is pathological, and this kind of limited regression may reflect flexibility and creativity.

Object Relations Theory

The concept of "object relations" in psychoanalytic writings of the last two generations means relations with significant others and their internal representations, starting with mother. Moreover, this approach emphasizes internal representations resulting from actual relations, and these representations as projected later on. Primitive, early object relations are the starting point for personality development.

> In broadest terms, psychoanalytic object-relations theory represents the psychoanalytic study of the nature and origins of interpersonal relations, and of the nature and origins of intrapsychic structures deriving from, fixating,

modifying and reactivating past internalized relations with others in the context of present interpersonal relationships. Psychoanalytic object-relations theory focuses upon the internalization of interpersonal relations, their contribution to normal and pathological ego and superego development, and the mutual influences of intrapsychic and interpersonal object-relations (Kernberg, 1976, p. 56).

According to this school of thought, personality is formed through object relations patterns which are set up in early childhood, become stable in later childhood and adolescence, and then are fixed during adult life, and reflected in transference patterns. The functioning of the adult personality depends on the maturity of one's object relations. Object relations theorists propose a personality structure and a drive system which are radically different from the classical systems. Thus, according to Guntrip (1969), the structure revolves around a central ego which is the "conscious self". It has various relationships with objects (external) and internal object representations. The ego seeks objects, and this is the basic drive animating the personality system.

While classical psychoanalytic theory viewed the personality as an information processing system, or a drive-based system, in touch (or out of touch) with reality, in object relations theory the emphasis is on introjection and projection, leading to a total distortion of reality. Compared with classical approaches, object relations theory is more pessimistic. It views personality as less reality-oriented, and its structure as determined earlier in life. One way of highlighting the differences between the two approaches is by looking at their concepts of a "critical period" in personality development. While in Freud's version the "critical period" in personality development is the Oedipal stage, here it is during the first year of life, when object relations patterns are determined.

The common core of instinct (i.e. classical) theory and object relations theory can be summarized in the two concepts of desire (for an object or for instinctual gratification), and separation (from the object or from life), through thanatos. Both approaches agree that our style of dealing with the world all starts with the small child and its (mis)understanding of sex, birth, family, with the resulting confused ideas that stay with us for life. Object relations theory says that the process starts very early, which means that the cognitive confusion is greater and deeper.

Historical Changes and the Study of Religion

Theoretical changes over time should have found their reflections and repercussions in the approaches to religion. Psychoanalysis has had more to say about religious actions than any of the various traditions in academic psychology. It is the one psychological approach to the understanding of religion which has exercised a major effect on both religion as an institution, and on the academic study of religion. Psychoanalytic approaches to the question of culture and religion, and to the question of individual integration in society, have affected all social science disciplines (e.g. 320). The psychoanalytic study of religious beliefs and institutions has drawn considerable attention from scholars in the fields of religion, history, sociology, and anthropology. Psychoanalysis is the only major psychological theory which offers an explanation of religion as part of a comprehensive theory of human behavior, in which religion is presented as an instance of general psychological forces in action (cf. Dittes, 1969).

FREUD'S WRITINGS ON RELIGION

Freud's contributions are the most ambitious attempt to date to present a comprehensive non-religious interpretation of religion in Western culture and history. The topics Freud dealt with include, first of all, a developmental theory of religion, both phylogenetically and ontogenetically. Freud also attempted to explain the functions and consequences of religion, for both society and the individual. Freud's theoretical explanation for the origin and existence of religion is based on certain presumed universal psychological experiences and processes: the universal experience of helplessness, the tendency for compensation through fantasy, and the experience of early relations with protective figures. Every individual is psychologically prepared by these universal experiences to accept religious ideas which are obviously culturally transmitted. The question about the world of spirits is: does this world exist "out there", and, if it does not, where is it. The psychological answer given by psychoanalysis is that it exists within, in our own mental apparatus and our own mental abilities to fantasize and project. The world of spirits, the supernatural world unseen and somehow felt in religious experience, is a projection of the internal world. Psychoanalytic theory explains both the origin of the supernatural premise and its specific contents.

Freud's theory does not suggest that the individual creates his religion *ex nihilo* as he grows up, but that childhood experiences within the family prepare the individual for the cultural system known as religion. Psychoanalysis sees every religious act, every religious belief or ritual, as an appropriate unit of analysis. There is no need for special sampling, since every unit of behavior is equally representative. The same basic method can be used to analyze a whole mythical system, or one individual believer. The psychoanalytic paradigm enables us to analyze both process and content in religion (cf. 334).

In this area, as in many others, Freud's writings offer a rich variety of hypotheses regarding various religious beliefs and practices. Some of the better-known hypotheses derived from psychoanalytic theory are the father-projection hypotheses (see 2101), the superego projection hypothesis (see 1901), and the obsessional neurosis hypothesis. These hypotheses can be interpreted both phylogenetically and ontogenetically. One thing that has to be remembered in connection with Freud's historical hypotheses is that explanations for the historical origins of religious acts may not be identical with or relevant to the motivation for such acts at present (i.e. it is possible that a certain religious act is a sublimation and ritualization of some prehistorical event or custom, but the person following this religious custom today is not aware of this origin and may be doing it for completely different reasons).

Going Beyond Freud

The psychoanalytic psychology of religion literature can be divided into two main parts: the original writings of Freud himself (see 334), and further contributions by his students and followers, such as those by Rank (1051), Reik (547), Jones (1513), La Barre (324) and Erikson (909, 1110). Among Freud's followers, Theodor Reik and Ernest Jones were those who followed him most closely, creating in effect essays in "applied psychoanalysis" by applying Freud's principles of interpretation to specific religious acts. Within psychoanalysis, newer theoretical conceptualizations have taken the place of the emphasis on Oedipal and instinctual motives, which has been typical of the psychoanalytic study of religion. The rise of object relations theory and the attention given pre-Oedipal experiences have broadened the scope of the basic psychoanalytic view of personal and cultural phenomena.

Object relations theory, arguably the most important theoretical development in psychoanalysis since Freud (1806, 1813), provides the best theoretical basis for understanding the world of spirits in relation to the internal world of objects. Rubenstein (337) complained about the research lag in the psychoanalytic studies of religion, which were still using the old instinctual framework while the newer object relations framework was already available. This gap is beginning to be closed now (e.g. 1811), and future work based on this approach promises to illuminate religion in all its varied manifestations. Quantitatively, psychoanalysis has contributed more to the psychology of religion than any other theoretical approach. More publications dealing with all aspects of religion can be identified with the psychoanalytic approach than with any other school or orientation. At the same time, the actual impact of the psychoanalytic approach is much more limited than could be expected on the basis of quantity alone.

A MODEL ANALYSIS

How can we characterize the psychoanalytic method of studying religion? Can we speak of a clear model? Several models were presented by Freud in his writings. The brief article titled "A Religious Experience", published by Freud in 1928, has remained a true tour de force, and one can easily imagine all authors wishing to come close to it in their work.

Methodologically, most psychoanalytic publications studying religious phenomena can be characterized by their structure and style. We can use the term "a model article", identified by several common characteristics. These include most often the choice of a ritual, myth or belief, cultural materials (sometimes in several cultures) to be discussed, rather than individual experience, and the use of material taken from anthropology, comparative religion, or archaeology. Often, clinical material is introduced after the analysis of historical or anthropological material to show parallels between individual and cultural processes. The model for this way of analysis is the clinical analysis of a dream or a symptom. The religious belief or behavior is selected as the segment of human action to be analyzed in order to discover an unconscious meaning, similar to the meaning of symptomatic behavior. The assumption is that religious acts are always psychologically meaningful and that the same rules apply to the analysis of individual and cultural products. The psychoanalytic style of studying religion becomes then very similar to the style of clinical discussion. Clinical material is used to validate interpretations of cultural products, because it is assumed that such material (dreams, free associations) leads us straight to the unconscious, to decipher its hidden language.

An excellent example of this model is the article by Walsh (1144). In this article a Hopi ritual, viewed as an institutionalized opportunity for acting out individual intrapsychic conflicts, is approached and interpreted with the help of materials taken from an ongoing individual psychoanalysis.

Another example is the article by Roheim (2006). Here an enormous number of anecdotes from European folklore, mythology, and African initiation rites, specifically genital mutilations, which all center on the notion of the phallic mother, are presented and interpreted together with clinical case materials.

USING CLINICAL DATA

How and why is the use of clinical data relevant and justified? Because both cultural rituals and individual associations, dreams, come from the same unconscious ocean of ideas and feelings, clinical data can be used together with ethnological data (e.g. 1135). There are permanent networks of ideation in the unconscious ocean of memory for both individuals and humanity (see 501). Any individual unconscious is part of the general human aquifer, a cross-cultural reservoir of unconscious ideas and urges that is tapped into in every case. A similar assumption is made in psychoanalytic biographies of religious leaders and of saints, which are in reality non-clinical extended case studies. These present us with serious problems of evidence and validation, familiar to students of what has been called psychohistory.

QUALITATIVE AND QUANTITATIVE ANALYSIS

The major qualitative characteristic of the psychoanalytic interpretations of religion is that they deal more often with the substance of religious beliefs and myths. Less often they deal with function and structure. Paradoxically, psychoanalysis, essentially a theory of individual personality, is less individualistic in its biases than other approaches, and this becomes clear when we look at the materials that have been used in psychoanalytic interpretations of religion, and which consist mostly of mythology, socially transmitted materials to which the individual responds. The literature of psychoanalysis, following Freud, has concentrated on religious mythology and ritual, rather than religious experience, as its subject matter. A quantitative analysis of psychoanalytic writings shows that mythology is a major topic, while religious experience receives less attention than it gets from other theoretical approaches. Of about 600 psychoanalytic studies listed in this book, less than ten percent have for a topic individual religious experiences. About fifty percent deal with mythology in one way or another, and the rest deal with dogma and ritual.

CRITIQUES

Criticism of the psychoanalytic approach to religion has been voiced often, not only from religionists, but also from sympathetic social scientists. One of the common complaints is the psychoanalytic tendency to over-interpret and over-psychologize, while neglecting the historical and cultural components of the phenomena under analysis. Of course, such accusations of "psychological imperialism" are made against psychological approaches in general from the perspective of other disciplines, and the avoidance of such imperialism should be a basic methodological concern to all psychologists.

Another kind of criticism, which is specific to classical psychoanalysis, is that it uses a model of psychopathology to explain the phenomena of religion, either as a substantive approach (phenomenon X is the expression of psychopathology, be it a "trance" state or a certain religious persuasion) or as an analogy (the dynamics of religious actions are identical to those of psychopathological symptoms — religion as a universal compulsive neurosis). To this criticism there are several answers. First, a dynamic approach to psychopathology means that underlying processes and forces are looked at, and they may be the same for pathological and non-pathological behavior. Second, there is a great deal of interaction between certain religious experiences and psychopathology, as clinical data indicate (e.g. 802). Third, there may be more psychopathology in individuals and cultures than they are ready to admit. The "neurosis" analogy for religion may be inappropriate for other reasons. It implies high ego involvement, which may not be present for most cases of "identity religion" (see 302), but only for a small minority of believers.

Many readers of psychoanalytic literature express their frustration with what seems like a mechanical and automatic application of classical Oedipal explanations. It seems that for any myth, dogma, or ritual, the practitioners of psychoanalytic exegesis are ready with the Oedipal template. What recent years have witnessed is that a mechanical application of a theoretical formula is not limited to the followers of the classical school.

Just like the stereotyped Oedipus explanations, we now find stereotyped object relations causality. For any myth, ritual or behavior, the explanation lies with bad mothering and/or early object loss (see 631). It is not that such explanations should be any more suspect than classical ones, but that they should be judged on their merits and the evidence presented to support them.

The Problem of "Psychoanalytic Archaeology"

Reik states "that the repressed in the history and prehistory of a people is really immortal and indelible" (1963, p. 23; see 1341). There are "eternal" psychological facts, which have to be uncovered. The assumption is that psychoanalysts are uniquely qualified to uncover the repressed, because they know how to use psychoanalytic tools. The reconstruction of ancient remote past is not exactly a job for psychoanalysts, and seems more appropriate for anthropologists and historians. Is there a place for archaeology? Yes, there is, when done by expert anthropologists, such as La Barre, Devereux, Dundes, and Spiro. Psychoanalytic archaeology should be read critically. Dilettante work cannot be justified, while the contributions by Reik and Roheim should be recognized for their originality.

Another common source of criticism is the use psychoanalysts make of historical and archaeological findings. There is little doubt that psychoanalytic works can be criticized on scholarly grounds, and that psychoanalysts may be poor scholars either in the application of their own theory or in their borrowing from other fields. Still, the weaknesses of specific applications may not negate the value of the general approach.

The tradition of historical speculation, initiated by Freud in *Totem and Taboo*, involves not only psychological hypotheses and questions, but also attempts to reconstruct ancient history, or pre-history. This is a reconstruction similar to that supposedly carried out in psychanalytic psychotherapy. Freud, in many of his theoretical writings, liked to use archaeological metaphors. Here the situation is turned around: not archaeology-like decoding of unconscious processes in psychotherapy, but real archaeological-historical research (second-hand). Speculations of this kind should be handled carefully, but here psychoanalysts have been quite careless, and most often, following Freud, have swallowed whole the Biblical conception of chronology and history, (i.e. from Abraham to Moses and to David as real persons and events).

This ancient mythology was taken at face value as history. In this case psychoanalysts have not exercised sufficient skepticism and caution and have fallen prey to cultural traditions.

In assessing the impact of the psychoanalytic approach on the psychology of religion in general one must consider facts both inside and outside of the psychoanalytic movement. Psychoanalytic studies of religion might have become more esoteric, because they are usually published in psychoanalytic journals, and are not usually read by the uninitiated. Their sphere of influence is thus limited. Some of the writings may be viewed as "sectarian" in the sense that one needs fairly esoteric knowledge, or one has to accept psychoanalytic working assumptions, but the effort is well worth it. Why does so much of this literature seem esoteric?

Some of the classical ideas suffer a degree of obscurity. More recent developments, and specifically the object relations school, are even more complicated. To truly appreciate a psychoanalytic article, the reader may need doctoral degree in social science and an extensive background in religion and psychoanalysis.

One piece of evidence regarding importance of the psychoanalytic interpretation of religion is the level of reactions to it by religionists and religious institutions. Psychoanalysis has been perceived as a major intellectual challenge to Western religion in the twentieth century. For religionists, psychoanalysis has remained a problem, as indicated by the number of books and articles written from a religious viewpoint and attempting to respond to that challenge.

OVERVIEW

After reviewing this large body of literature, we should have the right to ask whether it has really taught us something we did not know before, something we could not have otherwise known. The answer is clearly in the affirmative. Psychoanalysis has clearly led to a revolution in the study of religion in general and in the psychology of religion in particular. It has taught us many things we did not know.

When it comes to specific contributors and specific contributions, evaluation must be differential and careful. Some of the contributions are indeed of historical interest only, or may seem today even marginal historical curiosities. Some are clearly of enduring value for the psychological understanding of religion. As we read the individual contributions, one by one, we naturally tend to judge them by their creativity and originality. Do we ever feel, after reading an article, that we have learned a new way of seeing things that we had looked at many times before? There are indeed those unique moments when we feel while reading an original contribution that we have gained a real understanding of a phenomenon, something that before used to be beyond our reach. Enlightening, that is the greatest compliment to any psychoanalytic work, because that is the psychoanalytic ideal. Such a feeling may be rare, but it seems to me that at least a significant minority of the publications covered here reach that level.

Despite all critiques and criticisms, there is no substitute and no theoretical alternative to psychoanalysis, as the most, and the only, comprehensive theoretical approach to the psychology of religion. This is not a matter of belief or acceptance. Psychoanalysis is not a religious system. Despite many deficiencies, it is a good theory of religion not only for cases of high ego-involvement, but for explaining cultural commitments and the universal readiness for supernaturalism.

Significant changes and developments (if not true theoretical progress) over a period of almost a century are reflected in the literature. At the same time, some of the classical notions seem to be relevant and working for much material, many phenomena, and many believers. Going over the six hundred entries collected here, could I make a list of 100 "must read" contributions in the psychoanalytic tradition? My approach in evaluating contributions has been most critical. There will be those who might consider it too critical.

However, there are more than 100 items to be recommended wholeheartedly. This "hit parade" would include "oldies but goodies", as well as the latest in "adult contemporary", to follow the language of pop radio. These are my recommendations, but readers will have to judge for themselves.

In every section of the Annotated Bibliography, representing one content area, we can find more than just a minority of publications to be recommended. Thus, in Section 3 we find Eissler (309), Farrell (310, 311), Kovel (321), La Barre (322-325), Prince (333), Pruyser (334), and J.O. Wisdom (346). In section 5 we have Arlow (501), Bunker (509), Carroll (511), Fauteux (517), Ferenczi (519), Freeman (521), Gay (523), Henderson (524), Hutch (525), Jones (526, 527), Lowenfeld (532), Lutzky (533), Kaufman (528), Spiro (529, 566, 567) Klauber, Knight (531), La Barre (532), Muensterberger (538), Obeyesekere (539), Ostow (540-541), Parsons (542), Prince (543), Roheim (547-559), Reik (545, 547-548), and Ross (561).

In Section 6 we have Lubin (617), Medlicott (618), Misch (620), Obeyesekere (622), and Ostow (623, 625). In Section 7 we have Bychowski (705), Deikman (706), Ekstein (706),

Horton (719, 720), Lewin (721), Merkur (724, 725), Moller (726), Ostow (728,729), Paul (730), and Ross (732).

In Section 10 we have Arlow (1001), Deutsch (1017), Dundes (1019), Goldfrank (1024), Jones (1033), Merkur (1043), Rank (1051), Reik (1054-1057), Roheim (1058-1060), and Spiro (1064). In Section 11 we have Dundes (1108), Feldman (1112), Gay (1115, 1116), Jones (1121), Kiev (1123), and Roheim (1135). In Section 15 we have Breuner (1501), Carroll (1502-1504), Dundes (1504, 1505), Jones (1513, 1514), and Sachs (1519). We have sampled just a few of the sections, and we have found a true embarrassment of riches.

The quantity of recommended items is sufficient to demand the serious effort involved in examining them thoroughly. Their quality is sufficient to reward such an effort. These are such items which all scholars in disciplines studying religion should find stimulating, if not enlightening. Is this a tentative canon of psychoanalytic work on religion? Possibly, but a canon will be continuously selected by all scholars, and not by just one book.

In this book we have aimed at covering all relevant post-Freud publications. What we find is an incredible variety of views, with no unifying creed. Eighty years of Freudian inspiration and example have resulted in an impressive body of work. Freud's ideas have held an enormous attraction to many brilliant minds. Their effect has been that of a tremendous stimulus, but not a dogma, and not necessarily a model, as shown in the literature under review. Commentaries on Freud's writings are only a limited part of that literature. Most writings covered here are strikingly non-Freudian. Is there a "psychoanalytic school" producing interpretations of religion? Not exactly. There is only agreement on minimal basic assumptions, and the use of some elements specific to this approach (Oedipal extensions, ego-psychology, object relations).

Freud invented a way of "clinical" observation which we all want to imitate. Psychoanalysis has made a real contribution not only to the understanding of religion, but to the understanding of human culture and of humanity itself.

REFERENCES

Dittes, J.E. Psychology of religion. In G. Lindzey and E. Aronson (eds.) *The Handbook of Social Psychology*, Vol. 5. Reading, MA: Addison-Wesley, 1969.

Freud, A. *The Ego and the Mechanisms of Defense*. London: Hogarth, 1946.

Freud, S. Introductory Lectures on Psychoanalysis (1915/1916). In *The Standard Edition of the Complete Psychological Works of Sigmund Freud*, Vol 15. London: Hogarth Press, 1963.

Guntrip, H. *Schizoid Phenomena, Object Relations and the Self*. New York: International Universities Press, 1969.

Kernberg, O. *Object Relations and Clinical Psychoanalysis*. New York: Jason Aronson, 1976.

Rapaport, D. The structure of psychoanalytic theory. In G.S. Klein (ed.) *Psychological Issues*, Monograph 6. New York: International Universities Press, 1960.

Part 2
ANNOTATED BIBLIOGRAPHY

1

GENERAL SOURCES

1. GENERAL SOURCES

101. Beit-Hallahmi, B. *Psychoanalysis and Religion: A Bibliography.* Norwood, PA: Norwood Editions, 1978.

Now out of print, this systematic listing of about 800 entries, mainly in English, divided into 39 topics and indexed, has provided the best coverage of major works.

102. Capps, D., Rambo, L., and Ransohoff, P. *Psychology of Religion: A Guide to Information Sources.* Detroit: Gale, 1976.

This comprehensive bibliography of most of the literature on the psychology of religion to the 1970s includes very good coverage of classical psychoanalytic sources. Less than one tenth of the entries include brief annotations.

103. *Chicago Psychoanalytic Literature Index.* Chicago: Chicago Institute for Psychoanalysis, 1978-1988.

This source contains some useful references, but is limited in terms of classification and selection. It has been published irregularly.

104. Grinstein, A. *The Index of Psychoanalytic Writings.* New York: International Universities Press, 1956-1973. 14 vols.

This series is, and has been, the starting point for any serious work on the psychoanalytic study of religion. It does not eliminate the need for further work and has been superseded by newer reference books.

105. Meissner, W.W. *Annotated Bibliography in Religion and Psychology.* New York: The Academy of Religion and Mental Health, 1961.

This work is a classic, one of the most useful resources in the field, containing numerous entries relevant to psychoanalysis, with excellent annotations.

106. Rothgeb, C.L. *Abstracts of the Standard Edition of the Complete Psychological Works of Sigmund Freud.* (First mimeo edition: Rockville, MD: U.S. Department

of Health, Education, and Welfare, 1971) New York: International Universities Press, 1973.

This book is an amazing enterprise, seeking to summarize all of the *Standard Edition*. It is extremely clear and very useful. It is recommended not only for beginners, but also for the experts, providing essential summaries of everything written by Freud. There are useful indexes, but the coverage of religion here is limited.

For additional materials on this topic, see also 324, 334, 338

2
FREUD'S ORIGINAL WRITINGS

201. Barnes, F.F. The myth of the seal ancestors. *The Psychoanalytic Review*, 1953, *40*, 156-157.

    Evidence from folklore is used to buttress the notion of the primal horde. Since seals live in such hordes, where young males fight older ones for dominance, and some claim that people are descended from them, this is viewed as a projection of primal guilt. While it is clear that humans use animals as targets of projection, the interpretation is highly speculative.

202. Becker, E. A note on Freud's primal horde theory. *Psychoanalytic Quarterly*, 1961, *30*, 413-419.

    While recalling Freud's failure to meet the criterion of anthropological knowledge, the author salutes Freud's psychological penetration. Becker's reading of *Totem and Taboo* suggests that human cooperation became possible only with the development of a superego and symbolizing capacity.

203. Blum, H.P. Freud and the figure of Moses. *Journal of the American Psychoanalytic Association*, 1991, *39*, 513-535.

    Discusses Freud's preoccupation (or obsession) with the mythological figure of Moses. Over the years, Freud's writings on the subject are discussed in relation to various theoretical issues and his personal struggle with Jewishness.

204. Desmonde, W.H. The murder of Moses. *American Imago*, 1950, *7*, 351-367.

    This extremely speculative article starts with an acceptance of Freud's thesis in *Moses and Monotheism*, and then goes on to offer various fantasies derived from Biblical mythology.

205. Feldman, A.B. Freudian theology. Part I. *Psychoanalysis*, 1952, *1* (3), 31-52.

    The article presents, without criticism and at some length, Freud's view of the origins of religion and morality, as stated in *Totem and Taboo*.

206. Feldman, S.S. Notes on the "Primal Horde". *Psychoanalysis and The Social Sciences*, 1947, *1*, 171-194.

One traditional Jewish game and two Jewish rituals are interpreted as reflecting the perennial conflict between fathers and sons, and the persistent traces of the "Primal Sin" as related in *Totem and Taboo*. The author shows a good knowledge of Jewish culture, together with insightful interpretations, but the skeptics will not be convinced.

207. Fodor, A. Was Moses an Egyptian? *Psychoanalysis and the Social Sciences*, 1951, *3*, 189-200.

This essay contains a good analysis of Biblical texts, but follows closely and accepts uncritically both Biblical mythology and Freud's framework in *Totem and Taboo*. The final result is disappointing.

208. Fortes, M. *Totem and Taboo. Proceedings of the Royal Anthropological Institute of Great Britain and Ireland*, 1966, 5-22.

This survey of anthropological literature on totemism contains a brief critique of Freud's work. While rejecting the reconstruction of pre-history presented in *Totem and Taboo*, Fortes embraces wholeheartedly Freud's psychological insights regarding the connections between totem, taboo, and paternal authority.

209. Freeman, D. *Totem and Taboo*: A reappraisal. *The Psychoanalytic Study of Society*, 1967, *8*, 9-33.

After reviewing paleontological, anthropological, and ethological research on primate societies and traditions of totemism, the author has to be extremely critical of Freud's anthropological data. Freeman does not accept the idea of the "primal crime" as a reality, but as a psychological pattern, reflecting the force of aggressive and sexual drives within the nuclear family.

210. Gay, V.P. *Reading Freud: Psychology, Neurosis, and Religion*. Chico, CA: Scholars Press, 1983.

This volume consists of a unique commentary on Freud's major writings, including a major section covering the main writings on religion. It offers the reader numerous original and critical ways of looking at classical texts.

211. Jones, E. The inception of *Totem and Taboo. International Journal of Psychoanalysis*, 1956, *37*, 34-35.

Freud was quite ambivalent and dissatisfied with most of his publications. Among the few he was pleased with was the last chapter of *Totem and Taboo*, but even in this case he did express some doubts, and needed reassurances.

212. Jones, E. The birth and death of Moses. *International Journal of Psychoanalysis,* 1958, *39,* 1-4.

This article is a passionate defense of Freud's theses and speculations in *Moses and Monotheism,* written by a true believer.

213. Kroeber, A.L. *Totem and Taboo. American Anthropologist,* 1920, *22,* 48-55.

This early response on the part of academic anthropology stated clearly that there was no support from anthropological data for Freud's suggestions in this book. At the same time, it considered the book "an important and valuable contribution".

214. Kroeber, A.L. *Totem and Taboo* in retrospect. *American Journal of Sociology,* 1939, *45,* 446-451.

Following his earlier review [see 213], the author states that "There is no indication that the consensus of anthropologists during these twenty years (from 1919 to 1939) has moved even an inch nearer acceptance of Freud's central thesis". Still, Kroeber is ready to accept Freud's idea of the primal crime as a hypothesis, and to consider seriously some of the concepts introduced in the book. The universality of the incest taboo is accepted as one fact which supports the notion of Oedipal dynamics.

215. Lubin, A.J. The influence of the Russian Orthodox Church on Freud's Wolf-Man: A hypothesis. *Psychoanalytic Forum,* 1967, *2,* 145-162.

This is a speculative, detailed attempt to clarify some meanings in the Wolf-Man's symptoms and dreams, an addition to the literature on Freud's best known case (and therapeutic failure). It becomes clear that the symbolic world of Christianity in its Russian Orthodox form did indeed influence the Wolf-Man's private pathological world. It seems clear that religious symbols and objects should affect both normal and pathological mentation in any culture.

216. Malony, H.N., and North, G. The future of an illusion and the illusion of the future. *Journal of the History of the Behavioral Sciences,* 1979, *15,* 177-186.

This is a survey of the dialogue in letters between Freud and Oskar Pfister, which took place between 1908 and 1939. Their respective and opposing positions on religion are described and illustrated with excerpts from letters.

217. Mead, M. *Totem and Taboo* reconsidered with respect. *Bulletin of the Menninger Clinic,* 1963, *27,* 185-199.

The author speculates that Freud was, after all, right about the "primal crime", except that this deed was committed much earlier in the evolutionary history of humanity. It was a pre-human horde, when sexual maturity was reached at age seven or eight, and life was much shorter. And the deed was committed repeatedly, as each generation got rid of the earlier one over hundreds of thousands of years, until these pre-humans became real humans.

218. Paul, R.A. Did the primal crime take place? *Ethos*, 1974, *4*, 311-352.

An enthusiastic defense of *Totem and Taboo*, which suggests that Freud is falsely accused of espousing Lamarckian views in this book, although he did adopt them later on. The idea of the primal crime is taken seriously, but it isn't clear how far, and the reader is left wondering about the question stated in the title.

219. Reid, S. *Moses and Monotheism*: Guilt and the murder of the primal father. *American Imago*, 1972, *29*, 11-34.

Sets out to enlighten the reader about the puzzle of Jewish monotheism, by adopting completely first *Moses and Monotheism*, and then Biblical mythology regarding the history of the Jews in general (Moses and the settlement of Canaan as historical). The results fail to enlighten, and the puzzle remains.

220. Rosenfeld, E.M. The pan-headed Moses - A parallel. *International Journal of Psychoanalysis*, 1951, *32*, 83-93.

This speculative article starts with the acceptance of Freud's basic thesis in *Moses and Monotheism*, and then goes on to suggest various embellishments on Biblical mythology along the lines of the totemic sacrifice of Moses.

221. Slap, J.W. The genesis of Moses. *The Psychoanalytic Quarterly*, 1958, *27*, 400-402.

Attempts to extrapolate from clinical data in order to reconstruct the origins of the Moses myth, while accepting, just like Freud, the historical veracity of most of this myth. A good example of the combination of interesting clinical data together with unfounded speculations.

222. Smith, G.E. Freud's speculations in ethnology. *The Monist*, 1923, *33*, 81-97.

This is a serious critique of *Totem and Taboo*, coming from a scholar who admires Freud's overall contribution, and calls him "this great reformer". Freud is challenged on three main points: first, the existence of the primal horde, second, the commission of the primal sin, and third, "why one act, performed in one place, at one time, has had such tremendous repercussions"? Another point raised is that of Freud's confessed inability to explain the appearance of maternal deities, which had supposedly preceded the paternal ones.

223. Wallace, E.R. The psychodynamic determinants of *Totem and Taboo*. *Psychiatry*, 1977, *40*, 79-87.

The author interprets Freud's theories in a psychobiographical way, suggesting that he merely projected his own personal problems on the world. In his writings, Freud was expressing his own patricidal rage, elevating it to historical reality or a psychogenetic universal. He was also guilty of magnifying narcissistically the importance of his own psychic life, also exemplified by his identification with the mythological Moses. "Freud is alternately Moses the glorious father, Moses the victimized father, Moses the conquering son and parricide, Jesus the redeemer... Joseph the victim". Freud's devaluation of Judaism is also interpreted as a rejection of his father. As in all psychobiography, the value of such speculation is highly limited.

224.   Wangh, M. The genetic sources of Freud's difference with Romain Rolland on the matter of religious feelings. In H.P. Blum, Y. Kramer, A.K. Richards and A.D. Richards (eds.) *Fantasy, Myth, and Reality.* Madison, CT: International Universities Press, 1988.

Freud's famous exchange with Rolland around the notion of the "oceanic feeling", and its meaning, are explored here in a scholarly, stimulating, and scholarly manner. The dispute is interpreted in terms of both ideology and biography. It is concluded that the "oceanic feeling" refers to a merger with a loving, trustworthy mother. Rolland felt secure as an infant, while Freud probably did not, which determined later attitudes towards religion and death. This hypothesis seems worthy of further exploration in other cases.

For additional materials on this topic, see also 106, 327, 330, 332, 334, 342, 344, 345, 401, 402, 403, 407, 411, 433, 503, 510, 523, 523, 626, 711, 714, 723, 736, 1036, 1070, 1107, 1112, 1115, 1116, 1123, 1128, 1136, 1312, 1421, 1813.

And see Sections 3, 4.

3
CRITICAL REVIEWS AND OVERVIEWS

301. Apolito, A. Psychoanalysis and religion. *American Journal of Psychoanalysis*, 1971, *30*, 115-123.

This is a broad statement, emphasizing that to help clients in psychotherapy, the therapist must be sensitive to conscious and unconscious religious conflicts, which may be more common than we realize.

302. Beit-Hallahmi, B. *Prolegomena to the Psychological Study of Religion*. Lewisburg, PA: Bucknell University Press, 1989.

This brief survey of the state of theory and research in the psychology of religion presents psychoanalytic theory as the only comprehensive psychological theory available to those who are interested in a serious psychology of religious beliefs. Includes a review of the psychoanalytic approach, as well as theoretical and research suggestion stemming from it. Draws on psychoanalytic ideas to develop the notion of religion as a form of art and as a source for social and individual identity.

303. Brodbeck, A.J. Religion and art as socializing agencies: A note on the revision of Marxist and Freudian theories. *Psychological Reports*, 1957, *3*, 161-165.

Freudian and Marxian views of religion are classified as "cathartic" and criticized for ignoring the possible function of religion in "problem-solving". The stance seems to be that of the apologist for religion.

304. Burnham, J.C. The encounter of Christian theology with deterministic psychology and psychoanalysis. *Bulletin of the Menninger Clinic*, 1985, *49*, 321-352.

Despite attempted affinities, theological and psychological thinkers continued to clash over the issues of naturalism, reductionism, and determinism. Two institutional versions of interface, in the form of religious psychology and pastoral psychology, flourished in the middle of the 20th century, but overlapping functions as well as intellectual issues made even tentative cooperation uncertain.

305.   Casey, R.P. The psychoanalytic study of religion. *Journal of Abnormal and Social Psychology*, 1938, *33*, 437-452.

An interesting survey, reflecting sophisticated knowledge, which is outstanding for which chooses to offer instances of religion's capacity to create wholeness and cohesion in the life of children.

306.   Coles, R. *The Spiritual Life of Children*. Boston: Houghton Mifflin, 1990.

This survey of conscious, verbalized, religious ideation in children includes critical reflections on Freud's approach to the phenomenon of religion in general. Freud is accused of "gratuitous reductionism", and Coles offers instead a pro-religious view, which chooses to offer instances of religion's capacity to create wholeness and cohesion in the life of children.

307.   Day, F. The future of psychoanalysis and religion. *The Psychoanalytic Quarterly*, 1944, *13*, 84-92.

This is a critique of Zilboorg's well-known apologetic position, which aimed at a reconciliation of psychoanalysis and Catholicism. Day makes clear why such a reconciliation is impossible, and how much the Church (and any church) is threatened by the human sciences, more than by natural science. Articles published by Zilboorg before his conversion to Catholicism are quoted. A response by Zilboorg follows on pp. 93-100.

308.   Eisler, E.R. The religious factor in mental disorder. *Journal of Abnormal Psychology*, 1924-25, *19*, 89-95.

This article, which is only of historical interest, demonstrates that in the 1920s psychiatrists' notions of unconscious conflict, though influenced by psychoanalysis, were quite simplistic. The only original suggestion is that religious instruction may be a source of pathological ideation, and should be administered with great caution.

309.   Eissler, K.R. Extraneous dangers to psychoanalysis: Church and state; Appendix 2. Further notes on the religious controversy. In K.R. Eissler, *Medical Orthodoxy and the Future of Psychoanalysis*. New York: International Universities Press, 1965.

This is a lucid, erudite discussion of some critiques of psychoanalysis coming from religionists and their supporters (e.g. Erich Fromm). Eissler disputes the Roman Catholic Church and its various representatives who have criticized Freud's writings on religion, and shows that there is no common ground in this debate. There are also good discussions of some Freudian ideas, such as the analogy between religion and neurosis.

310.   Farrell, B.A. Psychological theory and the belief in God. *International Journal of Psychoanalysis*, 1955, *36*, 187-204.

By using the example of belief in fairies, Farrell demonstrates the implications of the psychoanalytic theory of religion, and ridicules all attempts at reconciliation between psychoanalysis and religion, and other kinds of contemporary apologetics. This article is important also for its general discussion of criticisms directed at psychoanalysis.

311.   Farrell, B.A. After Freud IV: Morals and religion. *The Listener*, June 21, 1956.

This text of a radio talk, honoring the Freud centenary on the BBC, is a model of lucidity and balance. The speaker, though critical of many Freudian notions, does judge them fairly and cogently. Regarding Freud's ideas on religion, Farrell raises two important points. First, he shows that characterizing a belief as wish-fulfilling does not prove it wrong. Second, and more important, any naturalistic analysis of religion, whether psychoanalytic or of other orientation, necessarily undermines religious beliefs and religion's authority.

312.   Flugel, J.C. *Man, Morals and Society*. New York: International Universities Press, 1945.

A classical exposition of classical psychoanalytic concepts regarding the super-ego and its effects on behavior. Regards religion mainly as a super-ego projection, and offers stimulating ideas about religious asceticism. May seem old-fashioned today, but contains many fresh insights.

313.   Gay, P. *A Godless Jew: Freud, Atheism and the Making of Psychoanalysis*. New Haven: Yale University Press, 1987.

Presents Freud as a loyal son of the Enlightenment, whose atheism was central to both psychoanalysis as an intellectual achievement and to the psychoanalytic view of religion. At the same time Gay demonstrates that there is nothing specifically Jewish about psychoanalysis, and demolishes any attempts to reconcile psychoanalysis with any religion.

314.   Groves, E. R. Freudian elements in the animism of the Niger Delta. *The Psychoanalytic Review*, 1917, 4, 333-338.

This early article is of historical interest only, and faithfully illustrates what was considered Freudian at the time, i.e. ancestor worship, paternal authority and insights into unconscious mechanisms.

315.   Heimbrock, H.G. Psychoanalytic understanding of religion. *International Journal for the Psychology of Religion*, 1991, *1*, 71-89.

Reviews classical psychoanalytic theory and its derivatives in ego psychology, object relations theory, and self psychology. It is argued that these approaches involve both hermeneutic and critical analyses of the unconscious as it manifests itself in religion. The article is marred by an apologetic bent.

316.   Homans, P. *Theology after Freud: An Interpretive Inquiry*. Indianapolis: Bobbs-Merrill, 1970.

Places both psychoanalysis and Protestant theology within the context of contemporary culture. Examines the effects of psychoanalysis on twentieth century

Protestant theology, and includes excellent summaries and analyses of Freud's basic writings on religion. Important for understanding religion in the age of secularization and the use of psychoanalysis in religious apologetics.

317.   Homans, P. *The Ability to Mourn: Disillusionment and the Social Origins of Psychoanalysis*. Chicago: University of Chicago Press, 1989.

This study views the development of psychoanalysis and the psychoanalytic approach to religion and culture within the context of secularization. The loss of unifying religious symbols started a long mourning process, with psychoanalysis being just one response to this loss.

318.   Hyman, S.E. The ritual view of myth and mythic. In J.B. Vickery (ed.) *Myth and Literature: Contemporary Theory and Practice*. Lincoln, NB: University of Nebraska Press, 1966.

Discusses favorably the Freudian approach, contrasted with Adler, Jung, Fromm, and Horney who are described as "cheery faith-healers". Suggests that psychoanalytic interpretations (including *Totem and Taboo*) are compatible with the ritual view, and with the study of myth in general.

319.   Kardiner, A. (with R. Linton) *The Individual and His Society*. New York: Columbia University Press, 1939.

This is an early exposition of the "culture and personality" school of psychoanalytic anthropology, dealing with religion as reflecting personality dynamics typical of a given culture. Early experience, especially parental discipline, will determine the content of religious beliefs and activities.

320.   Kardiner, A. *The Psychological Frontiers of Society*. New York: Columbia University Press, 1945.

This is a continuing exposition of the "culture and personality" school of psychoanalytic anthropology, containing examples of myths and rites as reflecting personality dynamics typical of a given culture. The analysis of religion as a projective system has to take into account cultural relativism. Since parental care varies in different cultures, the child's concept of the parents will similarly vary, and so will the resultant image of the deity. Not only are the images of the gods likely to vary in accordance with early concepts of the parents, but also the means of communicating with them and soliciting their help.

321.   Kovel, J. Beyond the future of an illusion: Further reflections on Freud and religion. *Psychoanalytic Review*, 1990, *77*, 69-87.

Freud's notions of religion as stemming from early experiences of the mother in the oceanic experience and to the father in the relationship to God-who-protects offer a cogent explanatory framework of the psychological side of religion. Criticisms of Freud's view are enumerated, and psychoanalysis is discussed as a response to an altered cultural climate. This is a lucid, important, contribution.

322. La Barre, W. Religions, Rorschachs and tranquilizers. *American Journal of Orthopsychiatry*, 1959, *29*, 688-898.

One of the best (and most spirited) short presentations of the psychoanalytic approach to religion. La Barre expresses eloquently and bluntly Freud's essential view of religion as infantile and neurotic, and applies it specifically to modern United States culture and to human culture in general. The mysteries projected by religions on the universe reflect our internal realities, which remain unknown.

323. La Barre, W. Geza Roheim: Psychoanalysis and anthropology. In F. Alexander, S. Eisenstein, and M. Grotjahn (eds.) *Psychoanalytic Pioneers*. New York: Basic Books, 1966.

This brief biographical study manages to combine admiration and criticism. It contains an excellent overview of Roheim's work and a sober evaluation of his lasting contributions.

324. La Barre, W. *The Ghost Dance: The Origins of Religion*. New York: Doubleday and Company, 1970.

This is one of the best articulated contemporary presentations of the psychoanalytic approach to religion. It combines Freud's classical theory with a rich collection of cultural and historical case studies. The basic notion is that of religious behavior as a neurotic reaction to stressful times. Suggests that the monotheistic god (one and eternal) is a denial of Oedipal wishes, because you cannot kill him and he does not have a wife you may covet, but the idea of god is also a projection of the omnipotent baby. The myriad of details and La Barre's amazing erudition may make the book forbidding for the uninitiated, but it can be used to advantage by selective reading of major chapters.

325. La Barre, W. Freudian biology, magic, and religion. *Journal of the American Psychoanalytic Association*, 1978, *26*, 813-830.

Freudian body-based psychology is peculiarly adapted to the needs of a holistic anthropology because it acknowledges the species-specific nature of the human body. The study of magic and religious behaviors is presented to exemplify a psychoanalytic-anthropological approach. While both analysts and anthropologists deal with naturalistic data, intellectual cooperation between them is problematic, (a) analysts have false fears that anthropological comparativism is their enemy; (b) analytic anthropologists are viewed with suspicion by both their colleagues and by analysts; and (c) fieldwork is often a naive unwitting autobiography. (d) Epistemological problems are shared by both fields because of the subjective nature of their data. It is suggested that, as in learning psychiatry one must encounter psychodynamics within oneself, anthropology must be learned in part from oneself and in part from experiencing the impact of the culture (as opposed to merely drifting along with it).

326. Lubin, A.J. A psychoanalytic view of religion. *International Psychiatry Clinics*, 1969, *60*, 49-60.

This is one of the best reviews of ego-psychology approaches, filled with many clinical vignettes, which illustrate the role of religious symbols in identification and personal adaptation.

327. Meissner, W. W. *Psychoanalysis and Religious Experience.* New Haven: Yale University Press, 1984.

An interesting and scholarly exposition of Freud's approach to religion, through a systematic survey of the original writings. In addition, Meissner presents many original ideas, strongly colored by an apologetic slant.

328. Meissner, W. W. *Life and Faith.* Washington, DC: Georgetown University Press, 1987.

Same as 327 in terms of basic ideas (many sections are verbatim repetitions of the earlier book), with additional materials which are purely theological and apologetic.

329. Michel, S. American conscience and the unconscious: Psychoanalysis and the rise of personal religion, 1906-1963. *Psychoanalysis and Contemporary Thought*, 1984, *7*, 387-421.

This valuable survey describes the influence of Freudian ideas on 20th-century liberal American Protestantism, focusing on two developments: pastoral counseling and religious family life education. Shows how Freudian notions were assimilated selectively, as psychoanalytic concepts were modified with spiritual doctrines, pragmatic philosophy, and the writings of the neo-Freudians. The contributions of writers such as Oskar Pfister and Karl Menninger are described.

330. Moxon, C. Freud's denial of religion. *British Journal of Medical Psychology*, 1931, *11*, 150-157.

An attack on Freud's *Future of an Illusion* and *Civilization and Its Discontents*, inspired by the theories of Otto Rank. Interprets Freud's rejection of religion as a reflection of his state of health and advanced age, as well as his personality, and compares organized psychoanalysis to an organized religion.

331. Pasquarelli, B. Psychoanalysis and religion - a postulated autonomy in function. *Bulletin of the Philadelphia Association for Psychoanalysis*, 1960, *10*, 10-17.

Sharply criticizes Gregory Zilboorg for his attempts to create a "syncretism" between psychoanalysis and Catholicism, and counsels a policy of complete separation between church and psychological theory or therapy.

332. Posinsky, S.H. Ritual, neurotic and social. *American Imago*, 1962, *19*, 375-390.

A fairly useful critique of Freud's approach to ritual as neurotic, to religion as neurosis, and to ritual in general, together with a review of approaches to ritual in anthropology and history.

333. Prince, R. Fundamental differences of psychoanalysis and faith healing. *International Journal of Psychiatry*, 1972, *1*, 125-128.

The differences between psychoanalytic treatment and faith healing lie in their basic goals. Psychoanalysis aims at insight and independence, while faith healing, by its nature, fosters dependence and faith.

334. Pruyser, P. W. Sigmund Freud and his legacy: Psychoanalytic psychology of religion. In C.Y. Glock and P.E. Hammond (eds.) *Beyond the Classics: Essays in the Scientific Study of Religion*. New York: Harper and Row, 1973.

This is a lucid and stimulating review, which must be read before starting any further work on Freud's writings. It is written from a critical perspective, and contains many original observations. Includes references and evaluation of writings which followed Freud's.

335. Rieff, P. The meaning of history and religion in Freud's thought. in B. Mazlish (ed.) *Psychoanalysis and History*. Englewood Cliffs, NJ: Prentice Hall, 1963.

A wide ranging discussion, informed by an equally broad erudition and historical-philosophical perspective. Imposing a model of religious thinking on psychoanalysis Rieff suggests that for Freud the Kairos, that crucial time in history, was the primal crime of parricide, as described in *Totem and Taboo*. Against the background of that Kairos developed both Judaism and Christianity, the first as the father-religion and the second as the son-religion, leading to competition and anti-Semitism.

336. Rieff, P. *The Triumph of the Therapeutic: Uses of Faith after Freud*. New York: Harper and Row, 1966.

A controversial reading of Freud's message and impact, with a presentation of a new cultural type, secular, self-critical and interested in his own well-being. This cultural type has developed in an essentially secular modern society.

337. Rubenstein, R.L. A note on the research lag in psychoanalytic studies in religion. *Jewish Social Studies*, 1963, *25*, 133-144.

This is a major review article suggesting that Freud (and his disciples) emphasized the phallic, the patriarchal, and the Oedipal in religion. It is further suggested that the following areas should now be explored (without disregarding the importance of the Oedipal): The underlying pre-Oedipal elements in patriarchal religions, the role of intrauterine regressive strivings, and the relationship between anality and the demonic.

338. Saffady, W. New developments in the psychoanalytic study of religion: A bibliographic survey of the literature since 1960. *The Psychoanalytic Review*, 1976, *63* , 291-299.

In the late 1950s, the psychoanalytic study of religion seemed to be in trouble. This was a result of reaching a dead end with the unimaginative application of exclusively Oedipal formulas. This article reviews contemporary publications, and reaches the conclusion that the psychoanalytic approach to religion has to rely on evidence gathered by anthropology and psychohistory, which is itself rather unreliable. Theoretically, it reports on changes in the direction of emphasizing pre-Oedipal factors, including the role of maternal images.

339. Schmidl, F. Problems of method in applied psychoanalysis. *The Psychoanalytic Quarterly*, 1972, *41*, 402-419.

An important discussion of "applied psychoanalysis", i.e. the application of psychoanalytic hypotheses to cultural products and historical developments, and its limitations. Includes a specific critical discussion of *Totem and Taboo* and its defective methodology.

340. Schroeder, T. The psychoanalytic approach to religious experience. *The Psychoanalytic Review*, 1929, *16*, 361-376.

This is a pansexual reading of psychoanalysis and of religion, suggesting that all worship was originally phallic worship, and all religious motivations are sexual in nature. The article is of historical interest only, to illustrate some early misreadings of Freud, as adopted by ardent anti-religionists.

341. Sherman, M.H. Values, religion and the psychoanalyst. *Journal of Social Psychology*, 1957, *45*, 261-269.

This wide ranging discussion offers an interesting historical analysis of the enmity between Freudian psychoanalysis and religion on the one hand, and the rapprochment between liberal religion in the United States and the culturalist school of psychoanalysis (Fromm, Horney) on the other hand.

342. Sullivan, J.J. Two psychologies and the study of religion. *Journal for the Scientific Study of Religion*, 1961-62, *1*, 155-164.

This is essentially a broad philosophical critique of psychological approaches to the study of religion. It focuses on differences between behaviorism and psychoanalysis as two possible approaches. While keeping his distance, the author praises psychoanalysis, prefers Freud over William James, and enjoys Erikson on Luther.

343. Taubes, J. Religion and the future of psychoanalysis. *Psychoanalysis*, 1956-57, *4-5*, 136-142.

Suggests that Freud's theory of the origins of religion, as put forward in *Totem and Taboo,* can be construed as a new theology of original sin and original guilt. Freud later expressed his preference for Christianity over Judaism, because of the former's contribution to expiating the eternal guilt. Nevertheless, Freud's position is cleanly atheistic, so that no such expiation is possible, as all religions are illusions. Thus, Freud, a tragic humanist, is one of the messengers of the post-Christian era. This is an original and eloquent reading of Freud's place in Western culture.

344. Wallace, E.R. Freud and religion: a history and reappraisal. *The Psychoanalytic Study of Society*, 1984, *10*, 113-161.

A critical review of Freud's original writings, which raises some major and cogent criticisms. First, Freud's lack of distinction between individual dynamics and cultural institutions. Second, the presumption of psychic unity not only across individuals, but over time and historical changes. States that accepting Freud's notion about the origins of religion in prehistorical totemism does not account for contemporary motivations and behaviors. Moreover, Freud's claims are being undermined by new findings in anthropology and archeology.

345. Wallwork, E. and Wallwork, A.S. Psychoanalysis and religion: Current status of a historical antagonism. In J.H. Smith and S.A. Handelman (eds.) *Psychoanalysis and Religion*. Baltimore: The Johns Hopkins University Press, 1990.

This chapter makes it clear again that a) Freud was definitely antireligious and b) the psychoanalytic view of religion, as of other human phenomena, is naturalistic. They remind apologists that "What psychoanalysis opposes is not illusion per se but lack of reflection about the unconscious wishes that enter into the creation of illusions and defensive opposition to critical examination of the works of the imagination with respect to their truthfulness " (p. 165).

346. Wisdom, J.O. Gods. In J.O. Wisdom, *Philosophy and Psychoanalysis*. London: Blackwell, 1952.

In an evaluation of psychoanalytic theory, written by a philosopher, Wisdom first demonstrates the limitations and even absurdities of philosophical debates about reasons for believing in gods. He then goes on to look at possible causes for belief in gods, and finds a confirmation of psychoanalytic ideas. That is because the feelings, and the stories, about various gods are indeed a continuation of how we felt as children, in relation to our parents and to adults in general. Moreover, the gods are also projections of our internal forces and desires, good and evil. This is an eloquent rendering of the psychoanalytic view.

347. Wulff, D.M. *Psychology of Religion: Classic and Contemporary Views*. New York: Wiley, 1991.

This is the arguably the best available, and most comprehensive, source about the work done in the field since the 19th century in both Europe and North America. About one-quarter of the text is devoted to psychoanalytic approaches, discussed fairly but critically. This book is simply indispensable for any future work.

348. Zock, H. *A Psychology of Ultimate Concern: Erik H. Erikson's Contribution to the Psychology of Religion*. Amsterdam: Rodopi, 1990.

This is a thorough, scholarly and comprehensive survey of Erikson's work, detailing every reference to religion. Summarizes the substantive contributions (religion as growing out of basic trust, religion and identity, religion and existential crisis) and some scholarly reactions. This book will remain the definitive work for the foreseeable future.

For additional materials on this topic, see also 222, 515, 523, 526, 537, 538, 544, 565, 1014, 1018, 1029, 1043, 1344, 1804, 1807, 1811, 1813, 1901, 2103.

And see Sections 1, 2.

4
FREUD'S JEWISH IDENTITY

401. Ater, M. *The Man Freud and Monotheism*. Jerusalem: The Magnes Press, 1992.

Most of this book is devoted to a serious, painstaking analysis of Freud's metapsychology. Its punchline is the claim that Freud's Jewishness played a role in everything Freud created. More specifically, it suggests that Freud was more ambivalent, i.e. more positive, in his attitude towards religion in general, and appreciated most its ethical significance. The author's most far fetched claim is that Freud intended to offer the world a revised version of Judaism, ethical and rational ("turning Judaism into a scientific theory"), and this was his intent in writing *Moses and Monotheism*.

402. Bakan, D. *Sigmund Freud and the Jewish Mystical Tradition*. Princeton, NJ: Van Nostrand, 1958.

This work attempts to tie psychoanalysis to Jewish traditions, and considers Freud's work to have a "kabbalistic" hidden character, but fails to prove its major point. The problem is that Freud had no connections with the specific mystical traditions in question. Bakan reports similarities between Freudian notions and ideas in the Jewish mystical tradition, but these psychological insights are probably found in many other cultures.

403. Bergmann, M.S. Moses and the evolution of Freud's Jewish identity. *Israel Annals of Psychiatry and Related Disciplines*, 1976, *14*, 3-26.

This is one of the most thorough and well-balanced reviews of the relevant evidence on Freud's Jewish identity. Both the positive and the negative feelings on Freud's part towards his Jewish background are examined, forming a picture of private ambivalence and public commitment.

404. Berkower, L. The enduring effect of the Jewish tradition upon Freud. *American Journal of Psychiatry*, 1969, *125*, 1067-1075.

This article surveys the influence of Jewish religion, broadly conceived as a cultural tradition, on Freud's work, without any detailed or penetrating analysis.

405. Blatt, D.S. The development of the hero: Sigmund Freud and the reformation of the Jewish tradition. *Psychoanalysis and Contemporary Thought*, 1988, *11*, 639-703.

The author attempts to demonstrate, without much success, that Freud's identification with the mythological patriarch Jacob exerted an important influence on the creation of psychoanalysis.

406. Bloom, H. Freud: Frontier concepts, Jewishness, and interpretation. *American Imago*, 1991, *48*, 135-152.

It is claimed that Freud's Jewishness was expressed in his passion for deep interpretations, leading to complicated theoretical concepts, such as body ego. This claim seems to be contradicted by the contemporary evidence of so many non-Jews who seem to follow a passion for interpretation.

407. Bruner, J. The (ir)relevance of Freud's Jewish identity to the origins of psychoanalysis. *Psychoanalysis and Contemporary Thought*, 1991, *14*, 655-684.

Suggests quite convincingly that Freud's Jewish identity bears no direct relation to the origins of psychoanalysis. Noting that Freud completely ignored ethnic identity when writing about psychopathology and came out against any claims for allegiance to Judaism, the author demonstrates that it ran counter to the zeitgeist of the late 19th century. Then, much was made of "degeneracy" within a racial context. The origins of psychoanalysis must be sought in clinical reality, not in any ethnic identity.

408. Cuddihy, J.M. *The Ordeal of Civility*. New York: Basic Books, 1974.

Suggests that the id in Freud's theory represents the 'Yid', the Jew from Eastern Europe, trying to gain emancipation and consciousness, and attempts to interpret Freud, as well as other thinkers of Jewish origin (Marx, Levi-Strauss), as reacting to Western "civility" by trying to unmask it and expose its dark side. This is supposedly the unconscious historical mission of psychoanalysis, as "social unease became mental dis-ease", and solace was offered for suffering Jews (and Gentiles).

409. Diller, J.V. *Freud's Jewish Identity: A Case Study of the Impact of Ethnicity*. Rutherford, NJ: Fairleigh Dickinson University Press, 1991.

Offers an important analysis of Freud's Jewish identity within the framework of what is known about ethnic group relations. Freud was a member of an ethnic minority, who did his best to adjust to a hostile ethnic majority. This experience, which is rather common in many societies, was traumatic. Majority negative attitudes are internalized, and this narcissistic injury leads to aggressive ambition. Freud's ambivalence about his Jewishness affected all of his writings about both religion and ethnicity.

410. Falk, A. Freud and Herzl. *Contemporary Psychoanalysis*, 1978, *14*, 357-387.

This discussion of Freud's Jewishness and his ambivalence about it contains much useful information, together with many speculations. It shows clearly that the home of Jacob and Amalie Freud was by no means the home of an observant family, and that Freud's exposure to Judaism was limited. It is shown that Amalie Freud ignored Jewish holidays, but held family gatherings on Christmas Day. This, together with other bits of evidence, indicates a considerable degree of alienation from Jewish traditions and Jewish identification.

411.   Frieden, K. *Freud's Dream of Interpretation*. Albany, NY: State University of New York Press, 1990.

The author claims that Freud ignored Jewish traditions and Jewish sources of dream interpretation in his own *Interpretation of Dreams* (1900), thus denying his own identity. He also criticizes Freud for his rationalist, atheist, position.

412.   Gilman, S. Translation in transition: The question of the *Standard Edition*. *The International Review of Psycho-Analysis*, 1991, *19*, 331-344.

Includes a fascinating analysis of Freud's theoretical discourse, and the development of psychoanalysis, as a reaction to anti-Semitic and racist ideas prevalent in the late 19th century. Jews were regarded as having an innate nature which was sexualized and corrupt. The sexuality was considered damaged and they were supposed to be susceptible to hysteria and insanity. They were considered degenerate and perverted, marked by genetic "inbreeding" and by the visible sign of circumcision, perceived as castration. Freud's reaction was to create a discourse in which sexuality and disease were universal.

413.   Grollman, E.A. *Judaism in Sigmund Freud's World*. New York: Block Publishing, 1966.

This article reviews the influence of Jewish traditions and images, and the inspiration Freud drew from some figures of Jewish mythology, and highlights anti-Semitism as significant in Freud's environment. The treatment is pedestrian and uninspired.

414.   Homans, P. A personal struggle with religion: Significant fact in the lives and work of the first psychologists. *Journal of Religion*, 1982, *62*, 128-144.

Presents the case of Sigmund Freud, together with those of Carl Rogers and Carl Gustav Jung, as examples of personal secularization and its effects on the formulation of psychological theories. What becomes clear from this analysis was that Freud's early life was much less affected by religion than those of Rogers and Jung. Freud never experienced an apostasy crisis, which the other two did.

415.   Ingham, J.M. Freud in a forest of symbols: The religious background of psychoanalytic anthropology. In David H. Spain (ed.) *Psychoanalytic Anthropology After Freud: Essays Marking The Fiftieth Anniversary Of Freud's Death*. New York: Psyche Press, 1992.

Here some Christian influences on Freud's ideas are considered, specifically Roman Catholic influences. Freud's biography is examined in detail, and correlated with theoretical points. Ingham states that Western culture "provided a supportive milieu for the discovery of the Oedipus complex and the elaboration of oedipal theory" (p. 157). Beyond that, it is hypothesized that Freud's Catholic nanny had a special influence on him and introduced the young Freud (at age three) to Catholic ideas. Much has been made of this nanny, and it is a measure of the obsession with Freud and his ideas, that so many fantastic claims are made about her. Ingham is quite critical in looking at the flimsy biographical evidence, which does not allow any sweeping conclusions. In a more serious vein he points out that Freud's reading of Oedipal impulses in religious traditions ignored the Jesus-Mary relationship, in favor of emphasizing father-son competition. This is undoubtedly correct, and is tied to Freud's reduced attention to pre-Oedipal attachments.

416.   Klein, D.B. *Jewish Origins of the Psychoanalytic Movement.* New York: Praeger, 1981.

Surveys much of the available evidence on the historical and social origins of psychoanalysis as an intellectual movement, and demonstrates its background in relation to the secularized Jewish European society of the time. According to Klein, Freud and his early followers regarded themselves as a Jewish elite, offering a new "redemptive hope" which was a "reinterpretation of Jewish redemptive vision". While being a generally reliable source, the book contains evidence of surprising lacunae in knowledge of Jewish traditions.

417.   Knoepfmacher, H. Sigmund Freud and the B'nai B'rith. *Journal of the American Medical Association*, 1979, 27, 441-449.

This brief historical survey shows that Freud was not only a regular member of the Vienna branch of the organization, but was quite active and involved in it.

418.   Krull, M. *Freud and His Father.* New York: Norton, 1986.

A detailed study of Freud's family background, with much information about his relatives and early environment. The main thesis, however, is totally speculative. It is that Jakob Freud underwent a crisis in his forties because of guilt feelings over his leaving Jewish tradition and breaking sexual taboos. Then Sigmund Freud underwent the same crisis in his forties, after his father died. This hypothesis cannot be proven and does not seem to add to our understanding of Freud's personal development or his theories.

419.   Loewenberg, P. Sigmund Freud as a Jew: A study in ambivalence and courage. *Journal of the History of the Behavioral Sciences*, 1972, 7, 363-369.

Explains one part of Freud's ambivalence about his Jewishness in Freud's wish to avoid being identified with Judaism or Zionism, aiming for the recognition of the universal value and validity of psychoanalytic theories.

420.   McClelland, D. *Psychoanalysis and Religious Mysticism.* Wallingford, PA: Pendle Hill, 1959.

The author sees the roots of psychoanalysis in "Jewish mysticism", and "cabbalistic thought" to which Freud was supposedly exposed during his childhood. The problem is that there is no evidence for such a claim.

421. Meghnagi, D. Jewish humour and psychoanalysis. *International Review of Psycho-Analysis*, 1991, *18*, 223-228.

This article relates the tradition of Jewish humor (often used by Freud) to the relationship between Jewish culture and psychoanalysis, but fails to contribute to any real understanding of the issue of Freud's Jewishness.

422. Meghnagi, D. (ed.) *Freud and Judaism*. London : Karnac Books, 1993.

This collection of literate and interesting essays, translated from the Italian, is animated by the proposition that Freud's work has been a cultural event within the Jewish tradition and the Jewish community. This idea clearly runs counter to Freud's own expressed views and wishes. The book also contains a previously untranslated lecture, given by Freud in 1915.

423. Miller, J. Interpretations of Freud's Jewishness, 1924-1974. *Journal of the History of the Behavioral Sciences*, 1981, *17*, 357-374.

This is an important survey of much of the biographical literature on Freud, suggesting that views of Freud's Jewishness, and the importance of this Jewishness for an understanding of his theory, have changed over time. The dominant view in the 1970s, as described here, is that of regarding psychoanalysis itself as the fruit of Freud's ambivalent position between modernity and tradition. This article defines some of the central questions in the debate over Freud's Jewishness.

424. Oehschlegel, L. Regarding Freud's book on Moses: A religio-psychoanalytical study. *The Psychoanalytic Review*, 1943, *30*, 67-77.

This is primarily an emotional defense of ancient scriptures, written by an ardent religionist but it contains one interesting idea: that Freud's strong identification with the Biblical figure of Moses has led him to claim that Moses was not really Jewish, because he himself would have liked to get rid of his Jewish identity, which caused him much difficulty throughout his life.

425. Ostow, M. Sigmund and Jakob Freud and the Philippson Bible. *International Review of Psycho-Analysis*, 1989, *16*, 483-492.

This article includes some interesting evidence is presented about the extent of Jacob Freud's knowledge of Hebrew (adequate) and of Sigmund Freud's exposure to Jewish learning (limited). Beyond the scholarly analysis of the Hebrew text of Jacob's 1891 birthday inscription to Sigmund, the data are over-interpreted.

426. Rice, E. *Freud and Moses: The Long Journey Home*. Albany: State University of New York Press, 1990.

Contends that Freud attempted an emotional and external departure from his milieu starting in early adolescence, and that towards the end of his life he began a return journey to religion in general and to Judaism in particular. More specifically, the book argues that Moses and Monotheism was an autobiographical work, and that it reflected an attempt to return to Freud's "Jewish roots". The evidence for this argument seems rather skimpy.

427.   Robert, M. *From Oedipus to Moses*. Garden City, NY State: Doubleday, 1977.

Interprets Freud's work as stemming from his ambivalence about his Jewishness, which was focused on his relationship with his father. The idea of the Oedipal situation reflected directly this actual relationship, and Freud's last published work, *Moses and Monotheism*, was a final attempt to resolve it. Freud's work as a whole is regarded as a Jewish response to modernity and to Freud's position as an outsider.

428.   Roith, E. *The Riddle of Freud: Jewish Influences on His Theory of Female Sexuality*. London: Tavistock, 1987.

The book claims that there were uniquely Jewish influences on Freud's work, which affected specifically his views of sexuality and of femininity. These represent traditionally Jewish perceptions. It is unclear whether these influences were unique to Jewish culture or were possibly prevalent in other cultures, or in European culture of his time.

429.   Rosenman, S. Psychological knowledge, Jewish identity, and German anti-semitic legends. *American Journal of Psychoanalysis*, 1982, *42*, 239-252.

Anti-Semitism was one of the challenges faced and overcome by Freud. Psychoanalysis, as a way of understanding stereotypes, both anti-Semitic and Jewish self-images, is a way of strengthening secular Jewish identity. This is an interesting and scholarly paper, and the idea of the need for a secular identity is cogent and important, but ignored by most students of the issue.

430.   Rubenstein, R.L. Freud and Judaism: A review article. *Journal of Religion*, 1967, *47*, 39-44.

This is a sympathetic, uncritical, review of Bakan (1958) and Grollman (1965), which tends to agree with Bakan's assessment of Freud as a "secularized Jewish mystic", despite the complete lack of evidence for it.

431.   Stewart, L. Freud before Oedipus: Race and heredity in the origins of psychoanalysis. *Journal of the History of Biology*, 1976, *9*, 215-228.

Interprets Freud's earliest work on hysteria (before 1890) as affected primarily by his opposition to the hereditary model, promoted by Charcot, which could have been (and was) used by anti-Semites. However, a reading of Freud's article on hysteria of 1888 shows him to be following still the same hereditary model. The change in Freud's views came later, and apparently had little to do with anti-Semitism.

432.   Vitz, P.C. *Sigmund Freud's Christian Unconscious*. New York: Guilford Press, 1986.

Like Bakan (see 402 above), Vitz seeks to connect Freud's theoretical view of religion to hidden biographical antecedents. But this time Vitz attempts to prove that behind Freud's atheism there was an early, unconscious attachment to Roman Catholicism, of all things. The attempt should leave most readers unconvinced, except those already committed to apologetics. The book is, nevertheless, scholarly and contains useful sources.

433.   Yerushalmi, Y.H. *Freud's Moses: Judaism Terminable and Interminable*. New Haven: Yale University Press, 1991.

This is a brief book which contains reflections, speculations, and re-readings of evidence regarding Freud's Jewishness. It analyzes *Moses and Monotheism*, and views it as expressing Freud's ambivalent attitude about Judaism, and about his own Jewishness. Yerushalmi claims that Freud suppressed the religious "fragments" of his life, while exhibiting in his work the essence of Judaic morality and civilization. He speculates that Freud, the godless Jew, as he called himself, might have wanted (in *Moses and Monotheism*, as well as in psychoanalysis in general) to leave his testament of godless Judaism.

For additional materials on this topic, see also 203, 223, 313, 317, 723, 1406.

5

ORIGINS OF RELIGION

501. Arlow, J.A. The consecration of the prophet. *Psychoanalytic Quarterly*, 1951, *20*, 374-397.

Several episodes of prophetic initiation and consecration, found in Biblical texts, are analyzed as hallucinatory-paranoid experiences, in which the voices heard are projections of the prophet's superego. The visions of God and contacts with him represent the fantasy of oral impregnation by the father, by ingesting his semen or feces. However, the prophet, like the artist, is capable of making these regressive experiences into important cultural messages, which are successfully communicated.

502. Bakan, D. *Slaughter of the Innocents*. San Francisco: Jossey-Bass, 1971.

Religious myths and rituals are interpreted according to a divergent explanation of the Oedipal situation. Here not the patricide drive is the motive, but the infanticidal impulse coming from the father. Religion was created by adults, and expresses the experience of the fathers, not of the sons. The myth of Jesus is seen as an attempt to make this infanticidal drive conscious. The mythological Jesus remains only a son, never a father. In the Roman Catholic Church, priests are "fathers", but also celibate, thus avoiding the danger of infanticidal impulses. The same impulses have been sublimated in Judaism through ritual circumcision.

503. Bergmann, M.S. The transformation of ritual infanticide in the Jewish and Christian religions with reference to Anti-Semitism. In H.P. Blum, Y. Kramer, A.K. Richards and A.D. Richards (eds.) *Fantasy, Myth, and Reality*. Madison, CT: International Universities Press, 1988.

This is an interesting and scholarly survey of the development of both Judaism and Christianity as reflecting the struggle against the infanticide impulse in fathers. This impulse and its sublimation is expressed in the Jewish Passover holiday, in the Christian Eucharist, and in the anti-Semitic blood libel against the Jews. The author presents his interpretation as an alternative to Freud's ideas about the development of the two religions, as presented in *Totem and Taboo*, which emphasize the same historical development of the two religions as reactions to the primal parricide. This is an important contribution, marred only by the readiness to take seriously some mythological notions.

504. Bomford, R.W. The attributes of God and the characteristics of the unconscious. *International Review of Psycho-Analysis*, 1990, *17*, 485-491.

Suggests that the concept of God in Christian tradition is a projection of the unconscious, as described by Freud through the attributes of eternity, infinity, displacement, condensation, and replacement of external reality by psychical reality.

505. Bonaparte, M. Psychoanalysis in relation to social, religious and natural forces. *International Journal of Psychoanalysis*, 1958, *39*, 513-515.

The fear of death, and the denial of death, are presented as the basic motives for religious faith. "One is a believer because one is especially afraid of death", and believers have a hard time facing their own mortality. Atheists, on the other hand, are able to adapt to reality, and psychoanalysis, being "that outstanding school for adaptation to reality", naturally leads to atheism. At the same time, it is pointed out that such realism is also a form of sublimated sadism.

506. Bonaparte, M. Universal myths. In S. Lorand (ed.) *The Yearbook of Psychoanalysis*. New York: International Universities Press, 1948.

Here we have grandiose and pessimistic speculations about the course of human history, written after the end of World War II. The only specific claim having to do with religion is that "young and triumphant religions [are], avid for the blood of the heretics who deny their creed". This, according the author, is the metaphor and the explanation for the Nazi death-camps.

507. Brody, M. Phylogenesis of sexual morality: Psychiatric exegesis on Onan and Samson. *New York State Journal of Medicine*, 1968, *68*, 2510-2512.

In reaction to the puzzling story of Tamar and the three brothers (see 1306), and the Biblical story of Samson, the author offers an elaborate, speculative, exercise in psychoanalytic archeology. He suggests that in prehistoric times, sexual behavior was regulated by a paranoid-phobic fear of defloration. This had survival value for the species, as young females were protected from predatory males. These fears were replaced by more humane rules with the coming of early Judaism, but vestiges and memories of early defloration fears and rituals are to be found in the Biblical text.

508. Brown, N.O. *Life Against Death: The Psychoanalytic Meaning of History*. Middletown, CT: Wesleyan University Press, 1958.

While the Freudian tradition has emphasized the Oedipal and the patriarchal in the formation of religion, Brown chooses to emphasize the role of anality in creating negative religious symbols. The demonic has taken the form of anal impulses in Christian tradition, as evidenced in the writings of Martin Luther.

509. Bunker, H.A. Psychoanalysis and the study of religion. In G. Roheim (ed.) *Psychoanalysis and the Social Sciences*. New York: International Universities Press, 1951.

This interesting contribution interprets religion as an attempt to overcome the Oedipal conflict through symbolic castration. If one is ready to give up incestuous and murderous wishes, then he is cleansed of "original sin" and rewarded with immortality. "Castration" must be the price of immortality.

510. Carroll, M.P. *Totem and Taboo*, Purity and Danger... and fads and fashions in the study of pollution rules. *Behavioral Science Research*, 1983, *17*, 271-285.

Discusses the theoretical explanations for pollution rules proposed by Freud, as compared to those offered by Mary Douglas in *Purity and Danger*. While the latter have enjoyed acceptance and popularity, Freud's explanations have been neglected. Carroll claims that Freud's analogy of individual phobia for the taboo has created a refusal to take it seriously, but holds that the notion of an unconscious attraction to the "polluting" object is indeed the key to the understanding of such taboos. Freud's theory of taboo should be treated separately from his thesis about the primal horde.

511. Carroll, M.P. *Moses and Monotheism* and the psychoanalytic study of early Christian mythology. *Journal of Psychohistory*, 1988, *15*, 295-310.

A brilliant, sophisticated, article, which rejects all pseudo-historical claims in *Moses` and Monotheism*, and selects for discussion only psychological hypotheses. Freud's hypothesis regarding the impact of childhood experiences and Oedipal resolution on the father image is discussed. It is then related to the differences between Judaism and early Christianity.

512 Casey, R.P. Oedipus Motivation in religious thought and fantasy. *Psychiatry*, 1942, *5*, 219-228.

This is a clear exposition of the classical psychoanalytic position, with specific interpretations of ancient Judaism and early Christianity. Points out that The Oedipus complex is unique in being normally and regularly suppressed rather than resolved, and thus having an enduring effect on the human personality. It is not surprising, then, that all religions contain projective fantasies which construe the "cosmic environment" in the shape of the family drama. Oedipal guilt is central to religion and is expressed in the Garden of Eden story, where opposition to the father and knowledge of the primal scene are followed by shame and punishment. The sense of sin, so typical of the devout, is the direct legacy of Oedipal guilt. Christianity offered a solution to that through identification with the sacrifice of Jesus.

513. Coriat, I.H. A note on the sexual symbolism of the Cretan snake goddess. *Psychoanalytic Review*, 1917, *4* 367-368.

This interpretation emphasizes the bisexual nature of the goddess, stemming from the essential bisexuality of the libido, which is expressed in many religious traditions.

514.   Desmonde, W.H. The eternal fire as a symbol of the state. *Journal of the Hillside Hospital*, 1953, *2*, 143-147.

The eternal sacred fire, common to many cultures, is interpreted as a vestige the murdered father's worship, symbolizing both the powerful sun and the father's wrath. Later on, it became a symbol of the state. At the same time, the fire may be a mother-symbol as well, and thus was symbolically bisexual.

515.   Endleman, R. Psychoanalysis and human evolution. *Psychoanalytic Review*, 1984, *71*, 27-46.

Presents a psychoanalytic-anthropological reconstruction of human evolution. The evolutionary process is viewed as being simultaneously both biological and cultural: More complex social organization, required by hunting, produced biological change, which then enhanced greater cultural development and more complex communication. These factors augmented group dependency, division of labor, sexual dimorphism, and prolonged infancy. Changes also occurred in sexuality, from a dorsal to a frontal position in coitus and from limited mating periods to the disappearance of estrus, with consequent nonperiodic sexuality. These developments led to the intensification of mother-infant erotic ties, the interplay of adult and infantile sexuality, the development of speech and language, and the rise of magic and religion.

516.   Erikson, E.H. *Childhood and Society.* 2nd ed. New York: Norton, 1963.

The focus in this well-known study is on the connection between developmental processes and social structure. Erikson offers a theory of developmental stages, in which religion is linked to the first stage. Religion is tied to basic trust and to the mother's role in creating (or not creating) that feeling. The banishment from the Garden of Eden, in the Genesis myth, is a reflection of the first ontogenetic catastrophe, which occurs with teething, and the eventual separation from the mother, creating a basic conflict between feeling of trust and evil.

Religious institutions reaffirm that sense of basic trust, which is necessary for normal development. "All religions have in common the periodical childlike surrender to a Provider or providers who dispense earthly fortune as well as spiritual health" (p. 225). Religions create faith, which is necessary for adults who need to create basic trust in their children.

517.   Fauteux, A. "Good/bad" splitting in the religious experience. *American Journal of Psychoanalysis*, 1981, *41*, 261-267.

The author suggests that early infancy splitting of the mother into good/bad object is reflected in religious belief systems about God and the Devil. The same splitting mechanism operates in converts to various new religions who reach a state of complete euphoria, denying negative impulses and negative realities, which are bound to resurface nevertheless. This is a lucid, important contribution.

518. Feldman, A.B. Freudian theology, Part II. *Psychoanalysis*, 1953, *1*, 37-53.

This article suggests that devotion to monotheism is the consequence of anal eroticism, because of the emphasis on rules and regulations, and rejects the theses of *Moses and Monotheism* as valid explanations for Judaism. This is certainly an interesting hypothesis.

519. Ferenczi, S. Belief, disbelief, and conviction. In *Further Contributions to Psychoanalysis*. London: Hogarth Press, 1926.

This brief lecture, originally delivered in 1913, treats both belief and disbelief as the consequences of early experience. It is the natural experience of every child to realize its own limitations, but to ascribe omnipotence to others surrounding it. Projection of this experience later on is the foundation for faith and gullibility. Disillusionment about the omnipotence and perfection of one's parents and significant others leads to scepticism, which may also take the pathological form of paranoia. It seems that psychoanalytic work since then has only followed these brilliant early insights.

520. Fox, R. *Totem and Taboo* reconsidered. In E.R. Leach (ed.) *The Structural Study of Myth and Totemism*. London: Tavistock, 1967.

The author argues that contemporary observations of primate social life and knowledge in evolutionary anthropology lend support to Freud's idea of the "primal horde". Among baboons one can find a social pattern of a troop with several dominant males, with young males being excluded from sexual competition. Concludes that the primal crime described in *Totem and Taboo* did occur, over and over, in horde after horde, and constituted a stage in human evolution.

521. Freeman, D. Thunder, blood, and the nicknaming of God's creatures. *The Psychoanalytic Quarterly*, 1968, *37*, 353-399.

Offers eye-witness observations of religious rituals in pre-literate tribes, which are interpreted as supporting basic Freudian notions. Thus, The gods of thunder and lightning are parent projections and rituals represents a variety of magical negotiations with the projected parent images, including symbolic damages to the genitals. Ideas of incest and preoccupation with the paternal phallus are reflected in taboo and myth.

522. Freeman, T. Some notes on a forgotten religion. *The Psychoanalytic Review*, 1954, *41*, 9-28.

Mithraism was a religion that once competed with Christianity for the status of the dominant religion in the Roman empire, and now is almost forgotten. Freeman's contribution in this article is not just in reminding us of this fascinating historical episode, but in offering psychoanalytic interpretations for Mithraic mythology and rituals. Following Freud and Roheim, the interpretations focus on the Oedipal complex. Mithraism is said to have provided psychical relief by neutralizing incestuous wishes and castration fears.

523. Gay, V.P. Against wholeness: The ego's complicity in religion. *Journal of the American Academy of Religion*, 1979, *47*, 539-555.

This article criticizes attempts to reconcile religion and psychoanalysis, and offers a brilliant reading of the ego's role in religion, following Freud's original writings. "Religious institutions have superego qualities but their core structure and their core function parallel the ego, not the superego... The ego's manifestation of repetition compulsion... is the dynamic core of religious institutions..." Becoming religious means that the ego acquires a ready-made defensive network, at the cost of giving up some reality testing, which means giving up its ability to confront the reality of suffering and death.

524. Henderson, J. Object relations and the doctrine of "Original Sin". *International Review of Psycho-Analysis*, 1975, *2*, 107-120.

This thoughtful, original article proposes that the doctrine of original sin, so central to Christianity, is a result of the psychological process of splitting, described by Melanie Klein. Splitting the object into 2 opposing parts, good and evil, which is said to occur in early infancy, is the result of the infant's having to face the opposing impulses of Eros and Thanatos. Psychoanalysis offers a solution to this eternal problem, through the recognition of evil within ourselves.

525. Hutch, R.A. *Religious Leadership: Personality, History and Sacred Authority*. New York: Peter Lang, 1990.

Offers a theory of leadership based on the concepts of Psyche (P), Society (S), and Culture (C), illustrated by such figures as Madame H.P Blavatsky, Mary Baker Eddy, Sri Aurobindo, and Elizabeth Kubler-Ross. It is suggested that the nub of sacred authority in life is a powerful mother-imago. Moreover, the experience of the sacred stems from the residuum, which is a carryover from the earliest psychological experiences. The residuum "is the psychological origin of all religious myths, rituals, doctrines, communities and ethics" (p. 85). "The residuum is the sum total of prototypical affect-laden traces or images... which, arising from infancy, remains the person's more or less fixed projection on the world and others" (p. 84).

526. Jones, E. The psychology of religion. *British Journal of Medical Psychology*, 1926, 6, 264-269. (Also in S. Lorand (ed.) *Psychoanalysis Today*. New York: International Universities Press, 1945. Reprinted in Jones, E. *Essays in Applied Psychoanalysis*. London: The Hogarth Press and the Institute of Psychoanalysis, 1951, Vol 2.

Jones presents here for the first time the clearest, and finest, psychoanalytic formulation: "The religious life represents a dramatization on a cosmic plane of the emotions, fears and longings which arose in the child's relations to his parents". This seminal statement can be seen as the beginning, and the inspiration, for much later work, especially in anthropology.

527. Jones, E. *On the Nightmare*. London: Hogarth Press, 1931.

This far-ranging survey of clinical material and cultural traditions seeks to demonstrate the connection between nightmares and a variety of supernatural beliefs. Some of the latter may be called superstitions and some myths, but the concern here is with their origins in experiences which are both individual and exceedingly common. The book contains many stimulating hypotheses regarding beliefs in devils, demons, and witches, and suggests that all such beliefs have their source in projections of unconscious ideas and conflicts.

528. Kaufman, M.R. Religious delusions in schizophrenia. *International Journal of Psychoanalysis*, 1939, *20*, 363-376.

Discusses materials taken from several cases, and presents the question of the apparent similarity between schizophrenic delusions and religious doctrines. Suggests that while individual delusions tied to paranoia lead to anti-social attitudes, religious beliefs, held by groups, foster sublimation, desexualization, and integration, within a social network.

529. Kilborne, B. and Langness, L.L. (eds.) *Culture and Human Nature: Theoretical Papers of Melford E. Spiro*. Chicago: University of Chicago Press, 1978.

This collection of 12 previously published papers includes 7 dealing directly with religion. Spiro is undoubtedly one of the most important contributors to psychoanalytically oriented work on religion, and each of his papers is of seminal quality.

530. Klauber, J. Notes on the psychical roots of religion, with particular reference to the development of Western Christianity. *International Journal of Psychoanalysis*, 1974, *55*, 249-255.

This is an important theoretical statement, one of the clearest to come out of the British object relations school. "Religious faith has its origins in the fantasies which the infant creates to justify its confidence that the mother will continue to protect and rule its world...the experience can be affirmed or revived only by symbolic means. The symbols have to be taken as literal truths because this provides the only means of conveying the truth of the experiences... The irrational components of religion - the swearing that nonsense is truth- is a test of social cohesiveness of a comparable kind".

531. Knight, R.P. Practical and theoretical considerations in the analysis of a minister. *Psychoanalytic Review*, 1937, *24*, 350-364.

An early (1935) case with fascinating analysis and conclusions. It offers first an understanding of the personality dynamics of the clergy, described as including narcissistic gratification (through the association with an omnipotent heavenly father) and outlets for aggressive drive "... for in the name of the Lord the minister can try to supervise and interfere with the lives of many of his fellow-beings". Regarding religious faith in general, while the author holds that religion is a "spiritualized solution of the Oedipus situation" and particular beliefs have many of the characteristics of schizophrenic delusions, he admits that faith can make life tolerable for many whom psychoanalysis will never reach.

532. La Barre, W. *Shadow of Childhood: Neoteny and the Biology of Religion*. Norman, OK: University of Oklahoma Press, 1991.

This is a brief recapitulation of La Barre's arguments regarding the origins of religion. Following Roheim and Freud, he suggests that prolonged human childhood, while adaptive in many ways, leads to the formation of illusory beliefs. Religion is classified not as a neurosis or a psychosis, but as an archosis, that is "an ancient and fundamental misapprehension about people or things that we have unfortunately acquired in learning our culture". Contains good discussions of crisis cults and of some modern illusions, such as the search for extraterrestrial intelligent life.

533. Leverenz, D. Shared fantasy in Puritan sermons. *American Imago*, 1975, *32*, 264-287.

This article analyzes Puritan theology, as reflected in published sermons. This theology turns out to be a system of ego defenses aimed at assuring survival. Imagery in the sermons is interpreted as based on early childhood fantasies.

534. Lowenfeld, H. The decline in belief in the devil - The consequences for group psychology. *The Psychoanalytic Quarterly*, 1969, *38*, 455-462.

This interesting discussion raises the question of historical changes in religious beliefs. The image of the devil arises from the ambivalence of the drives and the need to preserve the love object from hostile feelings. Thus a hate object is found, and hostility is projected on it, thus removing guilt. Belief in the Devil is part of monotheism, because the Evil One grew out of belief in many demons, but cannot really be easily reconciled with monotheism. It has been part of Christianity for 2000 years, but recently declined, depriving modern individuals of a ready-made outlet for fantasy aggression.

535. Lutzky, H. The sacred and the maternal object : An application of Fairbairn's theory to religion. In H.B. Siegel, L. Barbanel, I. Hirsch, J. Lasky, H. Silverman, and S. Warshaw (eds.) *Psychoanalytic Reflections on Current Issues*. New York: New York University Press, 1991.

This important and original contribution suggests that the "numinous" experience stems from early object relations, and proposes a solution to the mystery of the origins of the sacred. There is a connection between the sacred and the internal object, between early experience and the numinous.

Following W.R.D. Fairbairn, the internal object (world) is proposed as the prototype of the sacred. The dichotomies between the internal/external object and the sacred/profane are analogous, as the splitting of the maternal object and the ego is the prototype of the sacred/profane dichotomy. Moreover, the preservation of the bond with the mother by the constitution of the internal object as psychic structure is proposed as the prototype of the preservation of the social bond by the relation of the sacred to the social structure (cf. Durkheim). The individual phenomenology of the sacred is similar to the distortion of reality in schizoid pathology. The closedness of the internal object world is the prototype of the inviolability of the sacred.

536.   Mars, L. and Devereux, G. Haitian Voodoo and the ritualization of the nightmare. *The Psychoanalytic Review*, 1951, *38*, 334-342.

This is a speculative attempt, relying on etymology and some ethnographic data, to explain the origins of spirit possession in some cultures. It is suggested the tendency to ritualize the nightmare may have its roots in the cult of the Great Mother.

537.   Moxon, C. Religion in the light of psychoanalysis. *Psychoanalytic Review*, 1921, *8*, 92-98.

An early exposition of the idea of projection as the psychological basis of religion. "God is a product of the unconscious desire for a parental authority". Religious conversion occurs most often during puberty, when the need for a father substitute is greater, and ambivalence about fathers is reflected in the image of God as both loving and angry. Existential fears also play a role, and "... religion is a psychical flight from a dark and threatening reality ... to a state of infantile dependence".

538.   Muensterberger, W. The sources of belief: A reappraisal of Geza Roheim's theory of religious origins. Introduction to G. Roheim, *The Panic of the Gods*. New York: Harper, 1972.

"Who are the gods who panic? Who are the monsters and werewolves, ogres and witches? Or the bogeys, vampires, and vultures who appear in dreams and mysteries and threaten one's life? Whence those fears and figments; the notion of fantastic beings and domains no human is able to fathom? We encounter them everywhere. They are an integral part of the vast repertoire of human imagination, nay, the human condition. Their supernatural craft stems from that inspiration which in one way or the other belongs inevitably to everyone's childlike sense of impending doom or disaster and only magic, ritual, or prayer can tame or dispel" (p. ix). This is an excellent summary of Roheim's approach to religion, which focuses on early experiences as the origin of adult concepts.

539.   Obeyesekere, G. *The Cult of the Goddess Pattini*. Chicago: The University of Chicago Press, 1984.

This is a wide-ranging, meticulous, historical study with highly detailed analyses of texts and rituals. Its psychoanalytic sections highlight the similarities between the Pattini cult and other mother-goddess traditions. The pervasive myth of the mother-goddess (who is still a virgin) and the death and resurrection of her son (and often lover) is interpreted as expressing a wish to identify with the mother. This ultimate identification is achieved through castration, which in myth and ritual takes the form of various other bodily mutilations. While castration anxiety is tied to fear of (and identification with) the father, self-castration is tied to identification with mother.

540.   Ostow, M. Biological basis of religious symbolism. *International Record of Medicine*, 1958, *171*, 709-717.

Drawing on modern studies of animal behavior by Lorenz and Tinbergen, it is suggested that not only animals, but also humans may possess unconscious, innate control patterns, used to reduce aggression. The first is the display of vulnerability, which appears in Christian mythology and art. The second is the production of awe and subordination through ritual, and the third the cultivation of tranquility, practiced in Buddhism through meditation.

541. Ostow, M. The nature of religious controls. *American Psychologist*, 1958, *13*, 571-574.

Religion is presented as a major complex of instinctual control. To achieve control, the mechanism of regression in the service of the ego, as described by Kris, is utilized most effectively. Individuals in such a state become more compliant to religious authority as the edge of the pain of reality is blunted. The instinctual controls imposed by religion are only of relative value, and are far from totally effective, because of the power of instincts. At the same time, it is doubted whether secular controls are going to be used more wisely.

542. Parsons, A. Is the Oedipus complex universal? The Jones-Malinowski debate revisited, and a South Italian nuclear complex. *The Psychoanalytic Study of Society*, 1964, *3*, 278-328.

This original study suggests that the special pattern of family organization in Southern Italy, characterized by relative matricentrism, is correlated with a Mary-centered version of Christianity. This cultural reality coexists with an official pattern of patriarchy. Because of the relative weakness of the father in the real family, God the Father in the projective system of religion is secondary to the Madonna. Southern Italian men worship the Madonna and identify with Christ.

543. Prince, R. The Yoruba image of the witch. *British Journal of Psychiatry*, 1961, *107*, 795-805.

The cultural belief in witches and witchcraft, once prevalent in Europe, but now to be found only in traditional societies, such as the Yoruba, is interpreted to be a projection of infancy experiences. Following Melanie Klein, it is assumed that the infant passes through a stage of splitting the object into good one and bad one, occurring between the age of 3 months and 12 months. The idea of the witch is a projection of the bad maternal object.

544. Pruyser, P.W. *A Dynamic Psychology of Religion*. New York: Harper and Row, 1968.

This is an interesting, but not really successful, attempt to construct a new psychology of religion based on an eclectic version of ego psychology. At the same time, there is consistent and substantive reliance on classical psychoanalytic concepts.

545. Pruyser, P.W. *Between Belief and Unbelief*. New York: Harper and Row, 1974.

Starting with Winnicott's idea of transitional objects as the origin of illusion, the author proposes that each individual has a capacity for illusory experience, which determines a religious tendency or an ability for artistic creativity or art appreciation. Among people with such capacity, tastes develop for art, literature, religion, or ethics. Even ideals are transitional objects, and beliefs function as loved objects. This is a stimulating and original contribution.

546.   Pruyser, P. *The Play of the Imagination: Toward A Psychoanalysis of Culture.* New York: International Universities Press, 1983.

Suggests a model of three psychological worlds, each of which deals with fantasy differently : 1. the autistic world of uncontrolled fantasy and omnipotence; 2. the realistic world of reality testing and sense perceptions; and 3. the illusionistic world of tutored fantasy. The third world clearly includes religion as well as other cultural products. Religion is defined as " the illusionist enterprise par excellence". Here the author goes beyond his earlier works (see above 544, 545) to propose a brilliant integration.

547.   Reik, T. *Dogma and Compulsion: Psychoanalytic Studies of Religion and Myths.* New York: International Universities Press, 1951.

Reik suggested that the preoccupation with dogma, and all controversies and struggles around it, are reflections of unconscious doubts. Dogma is a defense mechanism, and the formulation of dogma is the result of two opposing obsessional ideas. The outcome is always a compromise between submission to dogma and rebellion. The example discussed is the dogma of Jesus Christ as the son of God and as God himself. This dogma was hotly debated, and bloodily fought over, for hundreds of years among competing groups in early Christianity. The resulting conception is seen as a compromise formation of obsessional, repressed and repressing tendencies, which expresses ambivalence towards both Father and Son. "Christ is not only present at the creation of the world but he himself creates the world at God's command. It is here that Christianity approaches most closely its unconscious goal-- the replacement of God the Father by Christ". The historical struggle over details was a displacement of the recurring doubts, ambivalence, and anxiety.

548.   Reik, T. From spell to prayer. *Psychoanalysis*, 1955, *3*, (4) 3-26.

This article suggests that the change from magic to prayer represents a decline in the belief in the omnipotence of thoughts, but this belief is still central to religion. This is an important and cogent observation.

549.   Roheim, G. *Australian Totemism: A Psychoanalytic Study in Anthropology.* London: Allen and Unwin, 1925.

Presents a large quantity of observation regarding totemism, incest taboos, and food taboos, in various Australian tribes. These are interpreted as supporting Freud's theory of the Totem, i.e. the totem is always a representation of the father, especially since beliefs held by these tribes seem to echo Freud's notions. In some tribes the origins of the totem are tied to incest taboos; in others the totem is considered an incarnation of the father, or a big brother.

550.   Roheim, G. The gods of primitive man and the religion of the Andamanesian Pygmies. *The Psychoanalytic Review*, 1928, *15*, 105-106.

Data about the religion of this traditional society are interpreted as supporting Freud's model of the creation of religion, as developed in *Totem and Taboo*. Connects the religious phenomena of totemism and monotheism. While monotheism stems from a repressed Oedipal conflict and expresses a fear of the dead father's spirit, in totemism this same spirit is projected onto the totem animal.

551.   Roheim, G. *Animism, Magic and the Divine King*. London: Kegan Paul and Co., 1930.

This is Roheim's *The Golden Bough*, a survey of beliefs and practices from numerous cultures and historical periods. From Australian tribes to ancient Judaic traditions and modern Christianity, magical practices are interpreted. They are all assumed to be growing out of both pre-genital and Oedipal concerns, especially castration fears. The book's contribution lies in reminding us not to be seduced by the idea of "higher" impulses in interpreting religious practices, as the latter can best be interpreted as related to our infantile fears and wishes.

552.   Roheim, O. Animism and religion. *Psychoanalytic Quarterly*, 1932, *6*, 59-112.

Based on field work in Central Australia, this article presents a theory of animism, which is viewed as having two poles, life and death, represented by souls and ghosts. While the ghost is derived from our death wishes directed against others and projected, the soul is the denial of death. Animistic beliefs and practices are interpreted as reflecting a phallic theory of the soul, and the soul leaving the body is a symbolic version of semen leaving the penis. Beliefs about ghosts, universally regarded as malevolent and vindictive, are interpreted as superego projections, (those are also the source of the idea of gods). Animism is the projection of the Oedipus complex in to the environment, and the abreaction of ego-superego conflicts in ritual, but animists do not have religion because they lack reverence or self-abasement. The creation of religion has to await a stronger superego and a stronger superego projection.

553.   Roheim, G. *The Riddle of the Sphinx*. London: The Hogarth Press, 1934.

This work is based on field work with the aborigines in Central Australia. It describes two co-existing religious systems. One is totemism, the religion of initiated men, official and esoteric. The second is based on belief in sphinx-like demons, represented by the medicine-man, and practiced by women and children. The demons are described as having huge genitals and cannibalistic tendencies. These images are the projections of the child's earliest anxieties, Oedipal as well as pre-Oedipal. With puberty and initiation, males move from demonology to totemism.

554.   Roheim, G. Primitive high gods. *Psychoanalytic Quarterly*, 1934, *3*, 1-133.

Field observations in the Andaman Islands and Central Australia are the basis for an analysis of religions in traditional societies. They are mostly interpreted in terms of neurotic, regressive, behavior. Observations are offered about the origins of religion in general: "It is because our infancy lasts longer than that of other animals that we need the supernatural beings". These beings are created by projection, but also by narcissistic identification.

555. Roheim, G. *The Eternal Ones of the Dream: A Psychoanalytic Interpretation of Australian Myth and Ritual.* New York: International Universities Press, 1945.

This is Roheim at his best, describing the complex ritual life of a "primitive" culture by looking at the hidden (and not so hidden) meaning of ritual and myth. These are all interpreted as growing out of early childhood experiences, distorted perceptions, and anxieties. What must strike the reader are the obvious similarities between such "primitive" traditions and the religious traditions we can observe right next to us.

556. Roheim, G. Mythology of Arnhem Land. *American Imago*, 1951, *8*, 181-187.

Mythological themes are analyzed at two levels, reminiscent of other publications by Roheim. One is Oedipal, and has to do with the killing of the primal father, followed by remorse and the creation of totemism. The other is pre-Oedipal, and has to do with early fantasies about the breast and the penis.

557. Roheim, G. *Magic and Schizophrenia.* New York: International Universities Press, 1955.

Roheim here defines magic "... as located somewhere halfway between the pure pleasure principle and the reality principle. If it were pure pleasure principle, hallucinatory wish fulfillment would be an aim in itself. If it were pure reality principle, we would set about and work to achieve a certain goal without assuming that our wish or dramatized wish is the thing that gets what we want" (p. 10). A third, *the magical principle* "...deals with the world outside as if it were governed by our wishes or drives or emotions" (p. 82). This is in reality the common manner in which we deal with the world. First, we believe we can do something and then we do it. Thus, an incantation followed by the actual killing of a crocodile with an axe proves and shows how magic works. The development of magical thinking is treated both ontogenetically, as superego appeasement, and dynamically as a defense against one's own aggression. The ritual of couvade is given as an example.

558. Roheim, G. The psychoanalytic interpretation of culture. In W. Muensterberger (ed.) *Man and His Culture.* New York: Taplinger, 1970.

At this stage of his research, Roheim was ready to reject a literal interpretation of the "primal crime" in *Totem and Taboo*, espousing instead a reading which sees it as a myth, reflecting the psychological reality of the Oedipal situation in every generation.

559. Roheim, G. *The Origin and Function of Culture.* Garden City, New York: Doubleday, 1971. (originally published in *Nervous and Mental Disease Monographs*, 69, 1943).

"The outstanding difference between man and his animal brethren consists in the infantile characters of human beings, in the prolongation of infancy...the immature

Ego evolves defense mechanisms as a protection against libidinal quantities which it is not prepared to deal with" (p. 17). This is how culture develops, and that is how cultural leaders evolve. All culture represents attempts to protect us from object loss. Sacred culture, as opposed to technology and science, is id- and superego-oriented, and represent institutionalized Oedipal fantasies. Certain individuals in each society become the carriers of sacred culture. Medicine men are "... the lightning conductors of common anxiety. They fight the demons so that others can hunt the prey and in general fight reality" (p. 51).

560.   Rosenzweig, E.M. Minister and congregation: A study in ambivalence. *Psychoanalytic Review*, 1941, *28*, 218-227.

This article is valuable today more as a historical-anthropological document, reflecting the experiences and insights of one Reform Judaism rabbi in the Northeastern United States in the 1930s. By way of psychoanalytic insights, it reminds us that the priest, to his congregation, is a father-surrogate which draws to himself all the ambivalence about the Father of Fathers and about the superego, internalized or external.

561.   Rubenstein, R.L. The significance of castration anxiety in Rabbinic mythology. *Psychoanalytic Review*, 1963, *50*, 289-312.

A preponderance of pre-Oedipal themes is found in ancient Judaic mythological literature. They are shown in fears of incorporation and drowning, rather than in castration fears. Moreover, it is suggested that the castration anxiety reflected in ancient Judaic mythology may represent a defense against more primitive fears of a devouring mother goddess, whose fertility rites often involved male genital mutilation.

562.   Rubins, J.L. Neurotic attitudes towards religion. *American Journal of Psychoanalysis*, 1955, *5*, 71-81.

Inspired by the theories of Karen Horney, the author differentiates between "healthy" and "neurotic" religion. He is opposed to the Freudian idea of father-projection, but his clinical examples, intended to illustrate the importance of social factors, still demonstrate the projection of family relationships onto the cosmic stage of religion.

563.   Schoenfeld, C.G. God the father and mother: Study and extension of Freud's conception of God as an exalted father. *American Imago*, 1962, *19*, 213-234.

Accepts the general outline of *Totem and Taboo*, though disagreeing with some details. Suggests that the concept of God may be not only a father-projection, as Freud has assumed, but also a mother-projection, based on our early childhood experiences, especially the importance of the mother in relieving anxiety. The young child probably hallucinates her presence in moments of great anxiety, which is the precursor of religious experience. So God is, in part, a mother-substitute, as well as a father-substitute.

564.   Skinner, J. Ritual matricide: A study of the origins of sacrifice. *American Imago*, 1961, *18*, 71-102.

Evidence from archeological, literary and historical sources is presented in an attempt to prove that the origins of religion and society was matriarchal. The Earth Mother was the object of worship, which included the sacrifice of human mothers. Self-castration and circumcision express identification with the mother and with the Great Mother. It is suggested that historical development of society and culture parallels the psychological development of the individual, in which early, pre-genital object relations play a central role.

565.   Spiro, M.E. Collective representations and mental representations in religious system symbols. In B. Kilborne and L.L. Langness (eds.) *Culture and Human Nature.* Chicago: University of Chicago Press, 1978.

A major theoretical treatment of the relationship between "official" religious doctrines and their meaning for individuals. Although religious systems are cognitive, they persist because of the powerful motivations and affective needs of individual actors. "Moreover, although the culturally constituted meanings of the symbols in which religious doctrines are encoded are consciously held by the actors, the latter also invest them with private, often unconscious meanings...".

566.   Spiro, M.E. Religious systems as culturally constituted defense mechanisms. In B. Kilborne and L.L. Langness (eds.) *Culture and Human Nature.* Chicago: University of Chicago Press, 1978.

This is a masterful statement of the relationship between individual needs and religious careers. Neurosis and psychosis are not the only means for resolving intra-psychic conflicts. There are other, more socially adequate ways of doing that. In addition, there are culturally constituted defenses, which serve to maintain the sociocultural system. In traditional societies, religion is the cultural system *par excellence* for achieving conflict-resolution. This is illustrated by the case of monks in Burmese society.

567.   Spitz, R.A. The genesis of magical and transcendent cults. *American Imago*, 1972, *29*, 1-10.

Proposes an explanation of the origins of religion through the distinction between magic and religion. Magical thinking is differentiated from ideas about transcendence. The latter are arrived at only when the father's role is conception, first experienced as a mystery, is realized. The father is perceived as contributing the Logos to the process of procreation.

568.   Suttie, I.D. Religion, racial character and mental and social health. *British Journal of Medical Psychology*, 1932, *12*, 289-314.

This psychohistorical, speculative article, attempting to reconstruct the pre-Christian culture of Europe, contains many original, stimulating, hypotheses. They cover such themes as the rebellion against mother-worship expressed in the rise of Protestantism, the status of women in pre-Christian times, the prominence of bother-sister incest in teutonic mythology, and Christianity as a psychotherapeutic movement. It suggests that there are four cultural solutions to the problem of incest: 1. matrifugal father cult (Judaism) 2. brother cult (early Christianity) 3. symbolic gratification through parental permission (Teutonic tradition), and 4. worship of the Virgin Mother Goddess (Catholicism). This last solution is unstable and forces the Church into a constant struggle with sexuality, resulting in celibate clergy and the doctrine of Immaculate Conception.

569. Tarachow, S. Ambiguity and human imperfection. *Journal of the American Psychoanalytic Association,* 1965, *13,* 85-101.

In this general discussion of ambiguity as a basic need of our imperfect ego, which focuses mainly on humor and art, religion is described as a way of offering an outlet for the instincts through ambivalence and ambiguity. Thus, in Catholic ritual God is both loved and eaten, i.e. destroyed. The survival of religion is explained through this ambiguous way of handling the sadistic and libidinal, similar to the process of artistic creation and enjoyment.

570. Vollmerhausen, J.W. Religion, perfectionism and the fair deal. *American Journal of Psychoanalysis,* 1965, *25,* 203-215.

The theoretical orientation here is inspired and framed by the ideas of Karen Horney, though they are by no means accepted without questioning. Religion is conceived of as a kind of neurotic claim, one of Horney's central concepts. It grows out of the child's helplessness and *basic anxiety,* another Horneyian concept. There is also a useful description of the magical thinking of children, which is highly relevant for discussing all religious thinking, including that of adults.

For additional materials on this topic, see also 202, 206, 217, 224, 320, 322, 324, 333, 337, 346, 401, 603, 607, 608, 627, 628, 630, 706, 711, 732, 820, 913, 917, 1013, 1017, 1020, 1022, 1051, 1054, 1064, 1066, 1104, 1106, 1107, 1111, 1117, 1123, 1319, 1330, 1339, 1342, 1344, 1513, 1518, 1519, 1603, 1609, 1806, 1807, 1811, 1813, 1814, 1901, 1910, 2008.

And see Section 3.

6

RELIGION AND INDIVIDUAL PSYCHODYNAMICS

601. Arlow, J.A. The Madonna's conception through the ear. *The Psychoanalytic Study of Society*, 1964, *3*, 13-25.

An identification with the Madonna brought about a fantasy of impregnation through the eyes in a young Christian woman, accompanied by hysterical symptoms. This case is used to illustrate the power of mythology in both reflecting and shaping character formation and unconscious conflicts. Theological arguments are shown to serve as rationalizations against unconscious guilt, as the wish to steal the phallus is transformed into the fulfillment of divine purpose. Thus, an ego maneuver leads id impulses to be integrated with superego and reality demands.

602. Atwood, G.E. On the origins and dynamics of messianic salvation fantasies. *International Review of Psychoanalysis*, 1978, *33*, 85-96.

Messianic salvation fantasies appear in individuals who have experienced one or more traumatic disappointments or losses in relationships with early love objects. Then, a regression to fantasy is followed by the developing image of the lost object as a deity. Later an identification with the lost object leads to the individual's declaring himself to be the saving messiah. The article is based on clinical cases of hospitalized individuals, but the dynamics described should be highly relevant to religious leaders (cf. 631 below).

603. Bowers, M.K., Berkowitz, B., and Brecher, S. Therapeutic implications of analytic group psychotherapy of religious personnel. *International Journal of Group Psychotherapy*, 1958, *8*, 243-256.

Offers unique insights into both the visible, human, side as well as the unconscious aspects of individuals who become ministers. Unconscious motivation include the need to overcome personal loss in particular as well as the fantasy of overcoming death in general. Omnipotence fantasies combine with helplessness and rationalization to make up a "clergy personality" type. These ideas may be relevant to theories about the origin of religion.

604.   Bowman, E., Coons, P., Jones, R., and Oldsrom, M. Religious psychodynamics in multiple personalities. *American Journal of Psychotherapy*, 1987, *41*, 542-554.

Comparing "primary" and "secondary" personalities, the authors report that "primary" personalities tend to believe in God, but are ambivalent about his nature, while "secondary" personalities have a clear-cut God image, which they reject. Conversion experiences were reported in 6 out of 7 cases. These findings should be interpreted against the cultural background of these individuals, and the problematic nature of the multiple personality phenomenon.

605.   Boyer, L.B. Christmas 'Neurosis'. *Journal of the American Psychoanalytic Association*, 1955, *3*, 467-488.

Suggests that depressions in adults, a common phenomenon around Christmas time, are an expression of reawakened sibling rivalry. The Christmas story brings back childhood traumas, as Jesus is sometimes experienced as a newly born sibling. Christmas depressions in females are characterized by penis envy, and a fantasy about receiving a penis as a Christmas present.

606.   Bozzuto, J.C. Cinematic neurosis following "The Exorcist". *Journal of Nervous and Mental Disease*, 1975, *161*, 43-48.

Several cases of hysterical "possession" following exposure to a popular film on possession and exorcism are analyzed. The dynamics are found to fit Freud's (1922) discussion of a "demonological neurosis". The individuals involved suffered from severe ambivalence towards a close relative or loss of that person.

607.   Carroll, M.P. Heaven-sent wounds: A Kleinian view of the stigmata in the Catholic mystical tradition. *Journal of Psychoanalytic Anthropology*, 1987, *10*, 17-38. (also in M.P. Carroll, *Catholic Cults and Devotions*. McGill-Queens Press, 1989).

The stigmata, which have appeared most often in Catholic females, are characterized by reported pain, observed recurrent bleeding, and reported inedia (persistent fasting). Classical psychoanalytic explanations suggest that stigmata represent hysterical behavior. Melanie Klein's theory, which assumes such complex processes as splitting and depression in early infancy, is offered as a substitute. It is hypothesized that the stigmata represent 1) the infant's desire to incorporate father, 2) the infant's desire for milk from mother's Good Breast, and 3) the infant's desire to make reparation for the imagined oral sadistic attack on mother. Looking at 5 documented cases of the stigmata, it is suggested that the imitation of the mythological Christ's wounds satisfies the desire for the father (that is why there are more such cases among women, and Catholicism involves "swallowing" the Christ). Bleeding is interpreted as expressing the desire for milk.

608.   Cohn, N., The cult of the free spirit: A medieval heresy reconstructed. *Psychoanalysis and the Psychoanalytic Review*, 1961, *48*, 51-68.

The history of a unique medieval religious movement is presented. This movement, in existence all over Europe, taught freedom from conventional morality and economy through the achievement of unity with God, following neoplatonic teachings. It was opposed to monogamy and private property, and advocated nudism. This episode is interpreted in psychoanalytic terms as expressing total regression to early childhood behavior and psychic functioning.

609.   Devereux, G. Belief, superstition and symptom. *Samiksa*, 1954, *8*, 210-215.

This article proposes some interesting theoretical ideas. It suggests that superstition is a magical display against magic aggression in which anal components are central. It can also serve as an expression of social rebellion.

610.   Eisenbud, J. Negative reactions to Christmas. *Psychoanalytic Quarterly*, 1941, *10*, 639-645.

Suggests that individuals' reactions to traditional holidays are determined by their personality makeup and unconscious conflicts, and not by the legends and rituals connected to any particular holiday. This is illustrated by two cases of women who reacted negatively to Christmas. This negative reaction was interpreted as stemming from the frustration of the wish for a penis, which Santa failed to deliver. Thus, religious traditions provide opportunities for individual projections.

611.   Erikson, E.H. *Identity and the Life Cycle*. New York: International Universities Press, 1959

An Individual's basic trust (or mistrust) is projected on the "cosmic order", creating the conditions for faith. Thus, it is early experience and basic trust, acquired during infancy, which are necessary for religious beliefs.

612.   Gilbert, A.L. The ecumenical movement and the treatment of nuns. *International Journal of Psychoanalysis*, 1968, *49*, 481-483.

This brief report is an eyewitness account of the effects of liberalization in the Roman Catholic Church in the 1960s. Following this historical change, some members of religious orders and the priesthood have left the religious life. The tie between official liberalization and the outbreak of intrapersonal conflict in individuals raises a question which goes beyond psychoanalysis and into social psychology: Does the liberalization of authority in an authoritarian organization lead to inevitable decline in individual commitment?

613.   Goodich, M. Childhood and adolescence among Thirteenth Century saints. *History of Childhood Quarterly*, 1973, *1*, 285-309.

This survey of historical documents points out that among most of these saints the mother was the dominant childhood figure, because the father was away from home, on crusades or secular business missions. This paternal deprivation led to an adolescence rebellion later on.

614.   Greene, J.C. A "madman" searches for a less divided self. *Contemporary Psychoanalysis*, 1969, *6*, 58-75.

A sympathetic analysis of a schizophrenic who seeks to struggle with his impulses and reach integration through the religious symbols which have surrounded him since childhood. This case study should lead to possible generalizations about personal integration through religion.

615. Jones, E. The God-complex. The belief that one is God and the resulting character traits (1912). In Jones, E. *Essays in Applied Psychoanalysis*. Vol. 2. London: Hogarth Press, 1951.

Describes a character type dominated by megalomania which reflected through excessive self-effacement and aloofness. The castration complex, which accompanies this character, expresses resistance to paternal authority and fear of the younger generation. Unconsciously, this is modeled after a God-idea, but consciously such individuals are atheists.

616. Kraus, F. A psychoanalytic interpretation of shamanism. *Psychoanalytic Review*, 1972, *59*, 19-32.

The shaman is "selected" and possessed (not demonically but positively) by a powerful spirit and undergoes a crisis which could be interpreted as a religious experience or a psychosis. Following this initiation period, the shaman is able to intercede on behalf of his tribe and its members with a variety of deities. Information gathered during "trips to heaven" enables the shaman to cure illnesses, predict the weather, and locate food, among other things. The shaman's behavior, analogous to a dream, is interpreted as a case of regression in the service of the ego.

617. Lubin, A.J. A boy's view of Jesus. *The Psychoanalytic Study of the Child*, 1959, *3*, 155-168.

A fascinating case study, based on an analysis of an adult masochistic homosexual, from a Roman Catholic family, who wished to change his sexual orientation (and reportedly did). In exploring the roots of his adult identity, it was discovered that a strong identification with Jesus, developed during the latency period played a major role. This was an identification with the mother, which became absorbed into a martyred, bleeding, feminine Jesus. There were also positive facets to this identification, which led to productive and warm social relations. The insightful exploration of elements in belief and ritual and the way they were processed and assimilated by this man (reminiscent of some Roman Catholic saints) should lead us to ask whether similar meanings are experienced by less deviant believers, and how.

618. Medlicott, R. St. Anthony Abbot and the hazards of asceticism: An analysis of artists' representations of the temptations. *British Journal of Medical Psychology*, 1969, *42*, 133-140.

This is an interesting contribution to the study of asceticism. The ideal of asceticism, which is not limited to "official" monks, involves regression, defective reality-testing, ego-splitting, and ego disintegration. Drives are distorted into masochism, activation of pregenital functioning, and substitute gratifications. Expressions of these processes are found in artists' works of all ages.

619. Meissner, W.W. The phenomenology of religious psychopathology. *Bulletin of the Menninger Clinic*, 1991, *55*, 281-298.

   Discusses the expression of various neurotic styles (hysterical, obsessional, depressive, narcissistic, and paranoid) through the vehicle of religious beliefs, suggesting that religious belief systems seem especially liable to serve as in the expression of neurotic tendencies and needs.

620. Misch, R.C. Impulse control and social feeling. *International Psychiatry Clinics*, 1966, *3*, 117-137.

   A fascinating case of a sinner who decided to become a saint, a bisexual transvestite who wanted to join a monastic order. Subjected to psychological testing, he was rejected by the order as a result, and then resumed the life of a sinner. His personality is interpreted with the help of the testing data, and he is described to have a harsh superego with gaping lacunae in it. This description may fit both exceptional saints and regular sinners.

621. Needles, W. Stigmata occurring in the course of psychoanalysis. *Psychoanalytic Quarterly*, 1943, *12*, 23-39.

   A 31-year-old man reported the first occurrence of stigmata (bleeding hands) after 5 months of analysis, and these reappeared twice later. The associations the analysand had related to masturbation, severe illness, or violence. Blood was always connected with semen, as the analysand had strong aggressive and homosexual tendencies, which he felt very guilty about. The analyst's conclusion was that the stigmata represented unconscious castration. This suggestion is directly relevant to the more than 300 reported stigmata cases since the 12th century.

622. Obeyesekere, G. *Medusa's Hair: An Essay on Personal Symbols and Religious Experience*. Chicago: The University of Chicago Press, 1981.

   This is an exercise in psychoanalytic anthropology, taking as its subject matter the deep motives of individuals committed to intense religious careers. The subject is Buddhist-Hindu ecstatic-ascetic religious virtuosi, whose matted hair reminds the observer of the mythological Medusa. The symbol systems they use combine idiosyncrasies and cultural traditions. Shows that the dramatic individual behavior of these ascetics is instrumental to their psychological stability, as well as to the survival of social structures around them.

623. Ostow, M. Religion and morality: A psychoanalytic view. In S. Post (ed.) *Moral Values and the Superego Concept in Psychoanalysis*. New York: International Universities Press, 1972.

   This chapter contains an original hypothesis about the relationship of religiosity to depressive states. It is suggested that personal movement towards greater religiosity is tied to a sense of depression. Religion is an antidote to depression, and as such is better than others, such as acting-out.

624. Ostow, M. Archetypes of apocalypse in dreams and fantasies, and in religious scripture. *American Imago*, 1986, *43*, 307-334.

Apocalyptic fantasies consist of two elements: first, the idea that the world will be destroyed, and second, that a remnant of humanity will be rescued from the catastrophe. These ideas appear in both schizophrenic or borderline individuals, and in religious scripture. This ideational pattern is traced back to its early childhood origins.

625. Ostow, M. Apocalyptic thinking in mental illness and social disorder. *Psychoanalysis and Contemporary Thought*, 1988, *11*, 285-297.

Apocalyptic thinking is defined as tied to the dynamic structure of the incipient psychotic episode, as in schizophrenia and borderline disorder. Libido is withdrawn from the world so that the latter disappears, to be replaced by a delusional fantasy of world rebirth. This chapter discusses the apocalyptic social movement, in which a charismatic leader inspires many individual apocalyptics.

626. Racker, E. On Freud's position towards religion. *American Imago*, 1956, *13*, 97-121.

Most of this article is devoted to the defense of "mature" religion, defined as the devotion to truth, justice, and beauty, and is of no interest to us. Its final section, however, includes an interesting analysis of atheism, especially in the case of Sigmund Freud. The grandiose image of Freud's father became a bad, persecuting image, leading to the fantasy of castration. Then starts the struggle against homosexual submission, idealization, and delusion, which leads to a complete denial of the father. Atheism in clinical cases is found to be connected to castration anxiety and paranoid reactions against homosexuality. Extreme hostility towards religion hides father-hate, father-love, and homosexual tendencies, as well as real disillusionment in relations with the parents.

627. Reik, T. The therapy of the neuroses and religion. *International Journal of Psychoanalysis*, 1929, *10*, 292-302.

This is an early discussion of religion as a practical, even "technical" issue in psychotherapy. Religious background of the analysand and his family has to be considered a potent cultural force, which affects individual neuroses. "Religion, as a collective repressive force, plays an important part in neurosis" (p. 298). The study of religion is presented as central for the conduct of psychoanalytic psychotherapy. It affects both resistances and what Reik calls the "unconscious sense of guilt" which is the "depth-dimension" of neurosis.

628. Schmidberg, W. Original sin. *Psychoanalytic Review*, 1950, *37*, 140-142.

The religious concept of original sin has been interpreted as reflecting guilt over parricidal or incestuous impulses. It is proposed that self-assumed guilt, to redeem a parent in the Oedipal situation, may really be the source. This is based on a case of psychoanalysis with a woman who had been in treatment with Freud himself.

629. Spero, M.H. Identification between the religious patient and therapist in social work and psychoanalytic psychotherapy. *Journal of Social Work and Policy in Israel*, 1990, *3*, 83-98.

This insightful and scholarly article reminds us that psychotherapy can bring about changes in the client's religious beliefs because of identification with the therapist. Such a process will be affected by aspects of the psychotherapy technique, such as therapist self-disclosure. Therapists are here advised against encouraging identification, and in favor of careful monitoring of its possible effects.

630. Spero, M.H. and Mester, R. Countertransference envy towards the religious patient. *American Journal of Psychoanalysis*, 1988, *48*, 43-55.

The human drive towards idealization is at the source of much religious and secular ideation. Psychotherapists, including psychoanalysts, may experience counter-transference envy reactions while treating religious individuals. This is especially likely when the psychotherapist is totally irreligious, or at least less religious than the client. This feeling of envy might rise from the unconscious or preconscious conviction that the clients, due to their religious faith, are free of existential doubts and emotional pains. Highly religious individuals (especially the newly-converted) may be perceived as self-confident and filled with inner strength and stability, sometimes claiming to be in a state of complete bliss. These perceptions are clearly countertransference reactions, reflecting the psychotherapists inner conflicts and wishes. The fascinating discussion of four cases presented here is highly relevant to projective reactions by non-therapists, who sometimes tend to idealize converts and highly devout individuals.

631. Stolorow, R. and Atwood, G. Messianic projects and early object relationships. *American Journal of Psychoanalysis*, 1973, *33*, 213-215.

Failed messianic projects, including those of personal commitment to a life of charity and religious devotion, result from an identification with an early lost object. The clinical case discussed demonstrates these dynamics. Jane, whose father committed suicide when she was 10, attempted to rescue others, and the whole world, but was bound to fail.

632. Wittels, F. A contribution to a symposium on religious art and literature. *Journal of Hillside Hospital*, 1952, *1*, 3-6.

In a posthumous publication, the author offers an original and important distinction between two types of religious experience: the hysterical and the obsessional. The hysterical is "prophetic" and emotional. Dogma and ritual are the obsessional aspect of religion. Both aspects are needed for a religious group to survive.

For additional materials on this topic, see also 215, 224, 308, 314, 320, 322, 333, 347, 510, 525, 528, 529, 531, 532, 544, 557, 559, 562, 570, 701, 702, 703, 704, 705, 708, 709, 714, 716, 718, 723, 727, 730, 734, 806, 809, 814, 818, 820, 903, 906, 908, 909, 910, 911, 913, 914, 915, 917, 918, 919, 920, 921, 922, 1030, 1115, 1116, 1120, 1139, 1320, 1330, 1414, 1512, 1603, 1604, 1802, 1803, 1806, 1807, 1809, 1810, 1811, 1814, 1814, 2104.

And see Sections 5, 8, 9.

7

RELIGIOUS EXPERIENCE

701.   Aberbach, D. Grief and mysticism. *International Review of Psychoanalysis*, 1987, *14*, 509-526.

The connections and similarities between mysticism and mourning are explored through testimonials, but mainly through literary works. Mysticism is said to provide an effective outlet for grief, satisfying the need for an orderly, goal oriented form of mourning. Severe childhood loss is found in the lives of many mystics, and of those who expressed mystical feelings in their poetry.

702.   Asch, S.S. Depression and demonic possession: The analyst as exorcist. *Hillside Journal of Clinical Psychiatry*, 1985, *7*, 149-164.

This clinical report describes, in line with earlier formulations, possession as demonstrating dissociative phenomenology together with evidence for underlying intra-psychic conflict and family psychopathology. Psychoanalytic treatment in this case is described as the exorcism of identification with introjected, ambivalently held objects.

703.   Bilu, Y. The taming of the deviants and beyond: An analysis of dybbuk possession and exorcism in Judaism. *The Psychoanalytic Study of Society*, 1985, *11*, 1-30.

The dynamics of spirit-possession in the Jewish tradition are explored using the records of all historically known cases. Possession is discussed as the articulation of sexual urges, and nonsexual aberrant impulses. The majority of the possessed were female, while the majority of spirits were males. At the social level, the deviance presented by possession is corrected by public exorcism, and community conformism is reinforced.

704.   Bilu, Y. and Beit-Hallahmi, B. Dybbuk-possession as a hysterical symptom: Psychodynamic and socio-cultural factors. *Israel Journal of Psychiatry and Related Sciences*, 1989, *26*, 138-149.

While exploring the culturally-determined idiom of possession in this Jewish instance, it is pointed out that the possession behavior is an acting out of deviant impulses, which include aggressive, sexual, as well as religiously antinomian ideas.

705. Bion, W.R. *Attention and Interpretation*. London: Tavistock, 1970.

This book contains a comparison of mystical experience and the psychoanalytic treatment situation, which turns into a confusing attempt to combine religious and psychoanalytic terms and treat them as equivalent.

706. Bychowski, G. The ego and the introjects: Origin of religious experience. *Psychoanalysis and the Social Sciences*, 1958, *5*, 246-279.

A significant theoretical contribution, which describes splitting as the basic and earliest ego mechanism. It in turn leads to a later yearning for unity, expressed through culturally defined religious experiences.

707. Deikman, A.J. De-automatization and the mystic experience. *Psychiatry*, 1966, *24*, 324-228.

Reported mystical experiences are explained in terms of changes in ego processes. According to Heinz Hartmann, the ego functions through automation of some perception and thinking operations. De-automatization of these operations may bring about the experiences of mystics who follow the traditions of contemplative meditation and renunciation. Thus, the mystical experience is one of internal perception brought about by changes in normal ego functioning.

708. Ekstein, R. A clinical note on the therapeutic use of a quasi- religious experience. *Journal of the American Psychoanalytic Association*, 1956, *4*, 304-313.

This is a unique case study based on an analysis of "Elaine," started at age 13, and continuing for at least 3 years. The diagnosis was borderline schizophrenia, and Elaine exhibited an unusual quantity and quality of (Christian) religious fantasies. This was interpreted as resulting from ego failure, leading to autistic and symbiotic regressions in the face of internal impulses and the transference situation. This is an *in vivo* example of the development of religious obsessions.

709. Fairbairn, W.R.D. Notes on the religious phantasies of a female patient (1927). In W.R.D. Fairbain, *Psychoanalytic Studies of The Personality*. London: Routledge and Kegan Paul, 1952. (also in *An Object - Relations Theory of the Personality*. New York: Basic Books, 1954)

A fascinating, moving, and poignant case study, which presents an unusual combination of sexual compulsion and religious fantasies. This unmarried woman became obsessed with both masturbation and religious visions, showing a typically psychotic picture. Fairbain correctly diagnosed this case as representing an extreme rarity among religious believers, but it might be less of a rarity among religious visionaries.

710. Fingarette, H. The ego and mystic selflessness. *Psychoanalytic Review*, 1958, *45*, 5-40.

This is a long and involved meditation on mystical states. Its theoretical thrust is an explanation in terms of ego psychology (contrasted here with "id psychology"). The loss of self claimed by mystics is interpreted as liberation from anxiety and functioning within the "non-conflictual portions of the ego". The way to achieve that is through controlled regression, which in some sense is compared to psychotherapy.

711. Fisher, D.J. Sigmund Freud and Romain Rolland: The terrestrial animal and his great oceanic friend. *American Imago*, 1976, *33*, 1-59.

Discusses the relationship and the correspondence between Freud and Rolland and their disagreement over religion. Rolland described his spontaneous feelings of religion as "oceanic", a description which haunted Freud as he composed the final draft of *Civilization and Its Discontents*. Rolland's three-volume work, *Essay on Mysticism and Action in Living India*, expounded on the 'oceanic feeling' and was critical of psychoanalysis. It seems that Rolland's criticism was a common one, that of differentiating between "personal religion" and "organized religion". Such claims have been made by other apologists since.

712. Greenacre, P. A study on the nature of inspiration. I. Some special considerations regarding the phallic phase. *Journal of the American Psychoanalytic Association*, 1964, *12*, 6-31.

Set within the framework of classical psychosexual stage theory, this is a classical explanation of the origins of the experiences of awe and inspiration. Thus, the phallic phase is described as the natural setting for experiences of revelatory significance. The increased motor ability increases the feeling of autonomy, and body functions are continually explored, especially genital ones. At the same time, there is a growing awareness of the outside world. Major discoveries of this period are expressed in vivid memories, which are projections of immediate experience on a cosmic stage. William Blake's reported experience of seeing God in the window at age four is interpreted as a possible projection of a genital discovery. Such creative projections occur, naturally, only among the uniquely gifted.

713. Harrison, I.B. On the maternal origins of awe. *The Psychoanalytic Study of the Child*, 1975, *30*, 181-195.

Awe, defined as reverential dread, is a basic element in religious experiences. While Greenacre (712) emphasized its phallic sources, this article suggests that the experience of the maternal breast and body as smothering or engulfing may also be a source of that feeling. A whole series of stimuli (parental intercourse, adult genitalia, menstruation, childbirth, death) may give rise to either dreadful or wondrous awe in the child. These suggestions are offered as extensions of Freud's ideas on oceanic feelings.

714. Harrison, I.B. On Freud's view of the infant-mother relationship and of the oceanic feeling - some subjective influences. *Journal of the American Psychoanalytic Association*, 1979, *27*, 399-421.

This article offers some interesting hypotheses about the biographical and psychodynamic differences between Romain Rolland and Freud, which in turn led to their different views of the "oceanic". Rolland denied the preoedipal "bad mother"and infancy traumas by adopting an hallucination of a divine mother, representing lost primary narcissism. Freud isolated childhood traumas through aversion, in his fear of merging with the ambivalent mother. The "oceanic" is the awe-inspiring maternal womb. This contribution is important not just because of the specific case studies, but because of its more general implications.

715. Hartocolis, P. Mysticism and violence: The case of Nikos Kazantzakis. *International Journal of Psycho-Analysis*, 1974, *55*, 205-213.

Mysticism may be a manifestation of conflict with one's own aggression, rather than with the violence of the outside world. Nevertheless, mystical impulses develop in societies which are outwardly peaceful, while encouraging violence. Regression under such conditions may lead to "demonic" experiences. The fascinating case of the writer Nikos Kazantzakis is presented to illustrate these suggestions.

716. Hartocolis, P. Aggression and mysticism. *Contemporary Psychoanalysis*, 1976, *12*, 214-226.

This article begins with an important review of the literature and then goes on to suggest that what pushes individuals towards mystical experiences is fear of their own aggression. This is illustrated with 3 case studies, and related to the conscious ideology of various new religious movements of the 20th century, which proclaimed peace as a response to, and denial of, the reality of internal and external violence.

717. Hood, R.W., Jr. Conceptual criticisms of regressive explanations of mysticism. *Review of Religious Research*, 1976, *17*, 179-188.

The author criticizes explanations of mysticism as "ego loss" because they supposedly assume a similarity of the mystical state to infancy psychological states. Such explanations were initiated by Freud and have are reflected in psychoanalytic writings, as well as in other approaches. Hood may not realize that the regression to infancy is conceived of as less than literal.

718. Hopkins, P. Analytic observations of the *Scala Perfectionis* of the mystics. *British Journal of Medical Psychology*, 1940, *18*, 198-218.

This is a review of mystical and meditation exercises in Western and Eastern traditions, including yoga, sufism, and The Jesuit order. These exercises are insightfully interpreted as related to pre-genital erotic impulses. The mystical path starts with suffering and the wish to start a new life. Confession, often the first step, is related to vomiting the bad inner objects. Yoga practices are interpreted as expressing mainly anal eroticism and auto-sadism. Its effects are regressive and auto-erotic. The strained posture it requires assures concentration and submission. More advanced stages on the road to perfection are compared to the stages of psychotherapy and viewed more positively. The mystical path ends in a reconciliation and union with the father imago. It starts with the sublimation of pre-genital drives, homosexuality and Oedipal guilt. This is a scholarly and fascinating contribution, a model of classical psychoanalytic interpretation.

719. Horton, P.C. The mystical experience as suicide preventive. *American Journal of Psychiatry*, 1973, *130*, 294-296.

This clinical article, using three examples of adolescents, contains an interesting and original theoretical idea: that the mystical experience itself may have the character of a potential transitional phenomenon (*vide* Winnicott). It becomes a "reliably soothing inner experience" that the individual may wish to return to with the help of psychedelic drugs.

720. Horton, P.C. The mystical experience: Substance of an illusion. *Journal of the American Psychoanalytic Association*, 1974, *22*, 364-380.

Denial and projected rage, resulting from the pain and disappointment of a ruptured symbiosis (i.e. pre-Oedipal), lead to mystical experiences. The mystical affective experience, sometimes accompanying conversion, is an attempt to repeat the transitional state, as conceptualized by Winnicott, through an upsurge of residual primary narcissism. It may be regarded as an adaptive ego defense.

721. Lewin, B.D. *The Psychoanalysis of Elation.* New York: International Universities Press, 1950.

Interprets states of elation as related to manic psychosis, and emphasizes regression to the early infant-mother symbiotic relationship in nursing. This regression creates the perception of fusion with loved objects in 'higher' mystical states, which are characterized by an indescribable ecstasy, and not by concrete visions.

722. Lutzky, H. Reparation and tikkun: A comparison of the Kleinian and Kabbalistic concepts. *International Review of Psycho-Analysis*, 1989, *16*, 449-448.

Points out similarities between Melanie Klein's concept of reparation and the Kabbalistic concept of tikkun. Suggests that the Kleinian concepts of the depressive position and reparation enable us to interpret the Kabbalistic myth, because the tikkun idea is a mythical cultural expression of the individual concept of reparation.

723. Masson, J.M. and Masson, C.T. Buried memories on the Acropolis: Freud's response to mysticism and anti-Semitism. *International Journal of Psycho-Analysis*, 1978, *59*, 199-208.

This needlessly complicated article contains one interesting idea: That mysticism is an affective illness, in which a person attempts to overcome depression by an unsuccessful regression to a happier past.

724. Merkur, D. Unitive experience and the state of trance. In M. Idel and B. McGinn (eds.) *Mystical Union and Monotheistic Faith.* New York: Macmillan, 1989.

Following a thorough review of the scholarly literature on mystical experiences, the author offers a sophisticated psychoanalytic theory of various mystical states. Trance states bring about defensive actions on the part of the ego, which takes the form of unitive experiences. Such unitive experiences are unconsciously produced compensations or defenses against mental paralysis. Personal mystical experiences reflect the ego and superego in communion, while impersonal mysticism is interpreted as a further manifestation of the superego.

725. Merkur, D. The visionary practices of Jewish apocalyptists. *The Psychoanalytic Study of Society*, 1989, *14*, 119-148.

This important study, based on impressive historical scholarship, includes an original hypothesis regarding the source of religious ecstasy. It is regarded as a result of the operation of the bipolar mood mechanism. When negative affects aroused by religion are unconsciously transformed into their bipolar opposite, the conscious sense of being forgiven and morally right is evidence of salvation. Such ecstatic induction techniques might have practiced by various religious visionaries. Apocalyptists' euphoria are regarded as superego phenomena, as it is the source of internal criticism and praise.

726. Moller, H. Affective mysticism in Western civilization. *Psychoanalytic Review*, 1965, *52*, 259-274.

Affective mysticism, a dominant phenomenon in Europe between the 12th and the 18th century, is analyzed here as a form of the sexualization of religion. Most of its practitioners were women, whose fantasies are easily recognized as reflecting basic conflicts which fit into the framework of classical psychoanalysis. Sado-masochism seems prominent in their reported experiences.

727. Moloney, J.C. Mother, God and superego. *Journal of the American Psychoanalytic Association*, 1954, *21*, 120-151.

The experience of theophany, or sudden enlightenment, is explained as the emptying of self-esteem into the superego,as the individual attempts to achieve security. Becoming a carbon copy of the superego, the person becomes part of the master's plan, gaining the master's protection. This is tied to the early experience in the person's life of an authoritarian mother-"god". Theophany is thus a regression to a precognitive stage, as the real self becomes dominated by the internalized superego-mother-breast.

728. Ostow, M. Antinomianism, mysticism and psychosis. In R.E. Hicks and P.J. Fink (eds.) *Psychedelic Drugs*. New York: Grune and Stratton, 1969.

Offers a comparison of mysticism and schizophrenia. Both are precipitated by an ambivalent situation, followed by a retreat from reality. In both cases the immersion in internal psychic life is interpreted as the experience of a hidden universe. The content of the mystical fantasy, psychically determined just like the schizophrenic fantasy, is that of a union with the beloved parent.

729. Ostow, M. Four entered the garden: Normative religion versus illusion. In H.P. Blum, Y. Kramer, A.K. Richards and A.D. Richards (eds.) *Fantasy, Myth, and*

Reality: Essays in Honor of Jacob A. Arlow. Madison, CT: International Universities Press, 1988.

Suggests that the "gnostic journey" represents an imagined return to physical intimacy with the mother, or with both parents. This may be in the form of a return to the mother's body, sitting in her lap, being in a parents' arms, or in the parental bed. Religious groups offering such journeys attract psychotics, depressives, and borderlines, as well as other escaping harsh reality. Speculates that organized religion, by offering " an illusion sponsored and controlled by the collectivity, tries to discourage irresponsible and self-defeating mysticism".

730. Paul, R.A. Fire and ice: The psychology of a Sherpa shaman. *The Psychoanalytic Study of Society,* 1988, *13,* 95-132.

Raises the theoretical question of discovering which childhood experiences are tied to the choice of particular religious roles. Here a case study of a shaman is presented in much detail. The man was a healer, and carried out a variety of magical tasks. His childhood included the early loss of parents, together with sexual traumata.

731. Prince, R. and Savage, C. Mystical states and the concept of regression. *Psychedelic Review,* 1966, *1,* 59-75. (also in J. White (ed.) *The Highest State of Consciousness.* New York: Anchor, 1972).

In this presentation of classical ego-psychology, the mystical state of "union" is interpreted as but a regression to an infantile level of experience, a return to the nursing situation. Whenever a self-described mystical experience brings about an improved functioning, it must be a regression in the service of the ego.

732. Ross, N. Affect as cognition: With observations on the meaning of mystical states. *International Review of Psycho-Analysis,* 1975, *2,* 79-93.

This is an important and lucid theoretical discussion. It suggests that the separation of affect from cognition is a developmental achievement, and in the infant their fusion is the rule. Mystical states involve regression to this infantile level of functioning, as indicated also by their characteristic narcissism. This regression is to the symbiosis with the mother at a pre-verbal stage, which explains the common claim of "ineffability". This regression is transient, otherwise we will have a complete psychosis. At the same time, no regression by an adult can recapitulate the infantile state, and it involves adult personality structures. Needless to say, such states cannot serve as guides to any reality outside themselves.

733. Schroeder, T. Prenatal psychism and mystical pantheism. *International Journal of Psych-Analysis,* 1922, *3,* 448-454.

This early contribution, of historical interest, interprets mystical experiences of a timeless and boundless being or union as the result of regression to an intrauterine state.

734. Seltzer, A. Psychodynamics of spirit possession among the Inuit. *Canadian Journal of Psychiatry,* 1983, *28,* 52-56.

Based on direct observations of clinical cases, this is a lucid report of possession as combining hysterical phenomenology and underlying intra-psychic conflict.

735. Sterba, R. Remarks on mystical states. *American Imago*, 1968, *25*, 77-85.

The author suggests that experiences reported as mystical states are the result of a regression to early infancy and its psychological processes.

736. Werman, D.S. The oceanic experience and states of consciousness. *Journal of Psychoanalytic Anthropology*, 1986, *9*, 339-357.

Surveys the history of the "oceanic feeling" in Freud's work and relates it to other approaches to mystical experiences. Offers an interpretation of that state as return to the early "undifferentiated self", a re-merger with the mother, combined with impulses from later developmental stages. The specific content of the experience is culture bound.

For additional materials on this topic, see also 347, 618, 622, 632, 806, 810, 912, 913, 1319, 1604, 1802, 1803, 1806, 1809, 1814.

And see Sections 6, 8, 17, 18.

8

CONVERSION

801. Allison, J. Adaptive regression and intense religious experience. *Journal of Nervous and Mental Diseases*, 1968, *145*, 452-463.

A study of sudden converts, compared to gradual converts, using the Rorschach, suggests that the former are better able to experience adaptively primary process thinking. The use of the Rorschach test raises questions of validity.

802. Allison, J. Religious conversion: Regression and progression in an adolescent experience. *Journal for the Scientific Study of Religion*, 1969, *8*, 23-38.

Based on an intensely studied case of adolescent conversion, a general conceptualization is proposed. Adolescent conversion is interpreted as changing the perception of the actual father as weak, ineffective, or absent, by creating an internal representation of a strong and principled substitute father, with clear values and firm judgment. This paternal image is crucial in helping the adolescent to achieve individuation and differentiation, and avoiding a sense of undifferentiated union with the maternal figure.

803. Apprey, M. Family, religion and separation: The effort to separate in the analysis of a pubertal adolescent boy. *Journal of Psychoanalytic Anthropology*, 1981, *4*, 137-155.

Presents the case of a 13 year old male who experienced a religious conversion to the Mormon faith while in psychoanalytic treatment. The treatment facilitated the boy's use of religious conversion as an adaptive transition from his earlier infantile object tie to its consequent renunciation and strengthened his identity as a young man with mature heterosexual ambitions.

804. Beit-Hallahmi, B. and Nevo, B. "Born-again" Jews in Israel: The dynamics of an identity change. *International Journal of Psychology*, 1987, *22*, 75-81.

Tested a group of 59 individuals, who had adopted Orthodox Judaism as a way of life after being raised in secular Israeli families, and compared them with a control group of matched individuals. The findings showed a lower reported level of identification with the parents among the 'converts'.

805. Bilu, Y. Jewish Moroccan "Saint impresarios" in Israel: A stage-developmental perspective. *The Psychoanalytic Study of Society*, 1990, *15*, 247-269.

This original study presents a previously unnoticed pattern of lifelong religious development, from early childhood to middle age and beyond, which is characterized by midlife conversion. This is interpreted as tied to changes in sexuality and fertility.

806. Bushman, R. Jonathan Edwards and Puritan consciousness. *Journal for the Scientific Study of Religion*, 1966, *5*, 383-396.

Edwards's conversion is cogently interpreted as a reconciliation with a great and terrible God, which was actually a reconciliation between father and son, and a resolution of an Oedipal crisis.

807. Cavenar, J.O. and Spaulding, J.G. Depressive disorders and religious conversions. *Journal of Nervous and Mental Disease*, 1977, *165*, 209-212.

This clinical study found a correlation between conversion and depression following ambivalence about the death of close relatives, older brother and father.

808. Christensen, C.W. Religious conversion. *Archives of General Psychiatry*, 1963, *9*, 207-216.

The interpretation here, based on clinical observations, follows ego psychology and the contributions of Erik Erikson. Conversion is viewed as an adolescent phenomenon, in which a weakened ego searches for, and finds, a way of integration.

809. Evans, W.N. Notes on the conversion of John Bunyan: A study in English Puritanism. *International Journal of Psychoanalysis*, 1943, *24*, 176-185.

This is another case study of a well-known historical personality. Bunyan is treated as a representative of Puritanism, based on his own descriptions in *The Pilgrim's Progress*.

810. Hitschmann, E. New varieties of religious experience: From William James to Sigmund Freud. In G. Rohelm (ed.) *Psychoanalysis and the Social Sciences*. New York: International Universities Press, 1947.

This study deals with several cases of conversion, counter-conversion, and religious struggles in adults, including Henry James, Sr., William James, Swedenborg, Franz Werfel, 3 anonymous cases, C.G. Jung, Albert Schweitzer, Schopenhauer, Gottfried Keller, August Comte, Selma Lagerlof, Knut Hamsun, Max Dauthendey, Goethe, and Soern Kirkegaard. The author's thesis is that "...the religious *Weltanschauung* is determined by the situation that subsisted in our childhood" and, specifically, the Oedipus complex which creates in individuals "...varieties of character types, neuroses, and different religious types". The ambivalence towards one's father is expressed through god images.

811. Kupper, H.L. Psychodynamics of the intellectual. *International Journal of Psychoanalysis*, 1950, *31*, 85-94.

This wide-ranging discussion of creative individuals (rather than 'intellectuals') includes an account of one case of conversion, which was well-publicized in the United States in the 1940s. Conversion is defined here as "regression... to a more complete disintegration of the ego". It is interpreted as a "complete breaking through of the repressed in so far as the pre-oedipal situation is concerned". In this particular case (Claire Booth Luce) there is also the development of a transference neurosis in relation to her 'converter', Fulton Sheen.

812. Levin, T.M. and Zegans, L.S. Adolescent identity crisis and religious conversion: Implications for psychotherapy. *British Journal of Medical Psychology*, 1974, *47*, 73-82.

The religious conversion of an adolescent male is viewed as an attempt to achieve ego integration, which improves its functioning, but is not capable of overcoming psychosis.

813. Lombillo, J.R. The soldier saint - a psychological analysis of the conversion of Ignatius of Loyola. *Psychiatric Quarterly*, 1973, *47*, 386-418.

The conversion of Ignatius, the founder of the Jesuits, is analyzed as a delayed identity crisis and resolution, occurring at age 30. The process was quite complicated, and it is compared to psychoanalytic "working through". The concept of "altered states of consciousness," which was fashionable in the 1960s, is also introduced, in the general context of ego psychology.

814. Masson, J.M. The psychology of the ascetic. *Journal of Asian Studies*, 1976, *35*, 611-625.

An insightful examination of the dynamics of this religious lifestyle. It finds that Indian ascetics have typically suffered one of three major childhood traumas: loss of a parent, seduction, or physical abuse. The resulting dynamics are one of extreme aggression towards internalized objects, expressed through the choice of an ascetic career.

815. Meissner, W.W. The cult phenomenon and the paranoid process. *The Psychoanalytic Study of Society*, 1988, *12*, 69-95.

Sources of psychological energy for the creation of deviant religious groups are found to reside in followers' personal difficulties, which are discussed in the language of object relations theory and psychoanalytic self theory.

816. Olsson, P.A. Adolescent involvement with the supernatural and cults. In D.A. Halperin (ed.) *Psychodynamic Perspectives on Religion Sect and Cult.* Boston: John Wright, 1983.

Adolescent preoccupation with "supernatural" objects is actually a mental representation of failed symbolic attempts to create separation from maternal and paternal objects. Three case studies are presented to illustrate this diagnostic generalization, whose validity may be supported by other reports.

817.   Salzmann, L. The psychology of religious and ideological conversion. *Psychiatry*, 1953, *16*, 177-187.

This theoretical review, supplemented by 4 interesting case studies, explains conversion experiences as a way of solving the conflict arising from hatred, resentment, and aggressive wishes toward the father, or anyone representing authority, including one's mother, and significant others in general. That is why the experience often occurs in adolescence.

818.   Spero, M.H. Clinical aspects of religion as neurosis. *American Journal of Psychoanalysis*, 1976, *36*, 361-365.

Discusses the treatment history of a 30-year old orally fixated man who became an orthodox Jew at the age of 20. This case is used to illustrate how religion can, in certain instances, be nothing more than a neurotic defense mechanism.

819.   Spero, M.H. Psychotherapeutic procedure with religious cult devotees. *Journal of Nervous and Mental Disease*, 1982, *170*, 332-344.

These individuals, who had undergone a conversion to minority religions, were characterized by severe ambivalence and an intolerance of this feeling and of any ambiguity, projections of hate and self-hate, and splitting. Work with them suggested that the elation following conversion is a manic reaction to depression. This is an insightful contribution.

820.   Spero, M.H. Aspects of identity development among nouveaux-religious patients. *Psychoanalytic Study of the Child*, 1986, *41*, 379-417.

The conscious rejection of the past in newly observant Jews is tied to feelings of shame and humiliation, while at the same time they believe to have been "chosen" for a special fate. These phenomena are lucidly illustrated in three clinical cases.

821.   Trosman, H. After the *Waste Land*: Psychological factors in the religious conversion of T.S. Eliot. *International Review of Psycho-Analysis*, 1977, *4*, 295-304.

A major force in twentieth-century literature who is also a case of conversion is analyzed with the help of biographical data and literary texts. There is evidence of unconscious aggressive drives towards Eliot's psychotic wife, as well as fears of a narcissistic merger with her. "An attempt at building psychic structure through maintaining contact with self-objects cathected with idealized cathexis". Vivienne, the wife, was evidence of failure. Religious conversion meant loyalty to royalty, nation and church, providing external supports against internal fears of fragmentation.

822.   Ullman, C. *The Transformed Self: The Psychology of Religious Conversion*. New York: Plenum Press, 1989.

This is an much expanded report on the research described in Ullman (see 1919 below), with additional theoretical discussion and case materials. The most significant determinant in cases of conversion is found to be the role of the father, and conversion seemed like a means of attaining an idealized father-attachment. Converts experience identification with the divine, a form of narcissism, because they wish to merge with an extension of the self.

823.   Weigert, E. The contribution of pastoral counselling and psychotherapy to mental health. *British Journal of Medical Psychology*, 1960, *33*, 269-273.

This brief article includes two important ideas. First, about the similarity between the religious rite of confession and secular psychotherapy, and then about the similarity between religious conversion and the profound change due to psychotherapy. The same mechanisms are said to be involved in both religious and secular change processes, based on transference, counter-transference, and trust.

824.   Weininger, B. The interpersonal factor in the religious experience. *Psychoanalysis*, 1955, *3*, 27-44.

Suggests that the main problem leading to religious conversion is not purely psychodynamic, but has to do with social difficulties. Conversion leads to group membership and belonging, thus reducing social isolation. Usually there is another person who acts as the catalyst in cases of religious conversion. Being accepted by that other person is crucial.

For additional materials on this topic, see also 347, 517, 537, 602, 604, 614, 620, 623, 630, 708, 709, 720, 721 727, 729, 905, 906, 907, 909, 910, 912, 913, 921, 922, 1603, 1604, 1919.

And see Sections 6, 7, 9.

9
BIOGRAPHIES

901.   Abraham K. Amenhotep IV: A psychoanalytic contribution to the understanding of his personality and the monotheistic cult of Athon. *Psychoanalytic Quarterly*, 1935, *4*, 538-569. Also in K. Abraham, *Clinical Papers and Essays on Psycho-Analysis*. London: Hogarth Press, 1955.

This is a well-balanced psychobiographical interpretation of the ancient Egyptian king who, under the name Ikhnaton, started a monotheistic religion 3000 years ago. The historical and archeological evidence is presented in great detail, and this version of early monotheism in the ancient Mediterranean is compared with later ones.

902.   Anderson, F.A. Psychopathological glimpses of some biblical characters. *The Psychoanalytic Review*, 1927, *14*, 56-70.

This early contribution exemplifies all the faults of eager interpretation of cases where no direct information is available. The author analyzes the mythological figures of Jacob and David in the Hebrew Bible, and the historical figure of Paul the Apostle. While Paul may be indeed historical, what we know about him is little more than legends. This does not stop the author from finding a "hysterical reaction" in Paul, "neurotic and psychopathic reactions" in David, and "incestuous fixations" in Jacob. Jacob's dream, as described in the Book of Genesis, is interpreted as a fantasy of an Oedipal triumph over the father.

903.   Bakan, D. Some thoughts on reading Augustine's *Confessions. Journal for the Scientific Study of Religion*, 1965, *5*, 149-152.

This is far from adulatory case study emphasizes Augustine's neurosis and follows an Oedipal frame of reference. It is the early relationship with the parents and the attempt to suppress sexuality that has formed Augustine's personality and was the source of all his energies.

904.   Berkley-Hill, O. A short study of the life and character of Mohammed. *International Journal of Psychoanalysis*, 1921, *2*, 316-53.

This is an early example of the use of psychoanalytic concepts in a biography of a religious leader. Speculates that Oedipal problems in Mohammed's early life were reflected later on in his religious doctrines, and presents much historical data to support its speculations.

905. Capps, D. Augustine as narcissist. *Journal of the American Academy of Religion*, 1985, *53*, 115-127.

Following recent developments in North American psychoanalysis, Capps proposes to view Augustine as a narcissistic personality, as defined by Heinz Kohut. If traditional psychoanalytic portraits of Augustine emphasized Oedipal problems, the analysis presented here is emphasizes pre-Oedipal personality development. What happened in Augustine's conversion should be described as a narcissistic transformation, rather than an Oedipal resolution.

906. Capps, D. *Hunger of the Heart: Reflections on the Confessions of Augustine*. West Lafayette: IN: Society for the Scientific Study of Religion, 1990.

This is an interesting collection of twenty reprinted articles, five of which are psychoanalytic in orientation. Most of the others, despite some theological biases, contain direct references to psychoanalytic interpretations.

907. Charny, E.J. The *Confessions* of St. Augustine. *Psychiatric Communications*, 1958, *1*, 101-111.

Based on the written text of the *Confessions*, various hypotheses are offered to account for Augustine's personality. The theoretical outlook is that of classical psychoanalysis, combined with Erikson's model of personality development. Most of the hypotheses seem insightful, except for several which assume that we can infer early infancy experiences from later behaviors. There are also interesting hypotheses about the relationship between Augustine's mother attachment and his theology, which centers on the Mother Church. Comparison with other religious leaders along the same lines should be fruitful.

908. Duff, I.F.G. A psycho-analytical study of a phantasy of St. Therese de l'Enfant Jesus. *British Journal of Medical Psychology*, 1925, *5*, 345-357.

The autobiography of a young French girl, born in 1873, who entered a convent at age 15, and died in 1897 of tuberculosis, is analyzed. Based on reported fantasies starting at an early age, the conclusion is reached that this girl was motivated by strong Oedipal wishes. The conflict over them was resolved by complete identification with the mother and the mother's genitals. Her vocation as a nun allowed a variety of genital and pregenital wishes a legitimate outlet.

909. Erikson E.H. *Young Man Luther, A Study in Psychoanalysis and History*. New York: W.W. Norton, 1958.

This biographical study analyzes the relationship between Martin Luther and his father during his identity crisis, and the subsequent change in his notions about God. Luther was driven very early out of the basic trust stage. His identity crisis in adolescence was a revival of the issues of the three early stages, with a renewed role for the father. Martin resolved his existential crisis while at the same time offering theological solutions for a historical crisis, in an example of creativity growing out of personal distress. The solution was the internalization of the father-son relationship, the establishment of an ego identity, the reaffirmation of basic trust, and the crystallization of individual conscience. This study has been severely criticized by historians, who disputed the historicity or the importance of most of the central incidents.

910. Erikson, E.H. *Gandhi's Truth: On the Origins of Militant Nonviolence*. New York: W.W. Norton, 1968.

This biographical study analyzes Gandhi's leadership qualities and suggests that they grew out of his personal identity development. The biographical evidence leads Erikson to conclude that Gandhi was deeply influenced by his mother's religiosity, and was very ambivalent about his father. Internal struggles about authority and impulses were overcome through the achievement of a clear identity.

911. Gay, V.P. Augustine: The reader as selfobject. *Journal for the Scientific Study of Religion*, 1986, *25*, 64-75.

Drawing upon psychoanalytic concepts starting with Freud's and ending with Kohut, this reading of Augustine goes beyond Oedipal and pre-Oedipal concerns, which are recognized, but not focused on. According to the present reading, it is to solve his self-concerns that Augustine turns to both his imagined God and his imagined readers.

912. Kakar, S. *The Analyst and the Mystic: Psychoanalytic Reflections on Religion and Mysticism*. Chicago: The University of Chicago Press, 1991.

This brief and lucid volume focuses on one case study of a "religious genius", the nineteenth century Bengali mystic Sri Ramakrishna. Kakar leaves behind our conventional diagnostic categories, and states that visions are "... not hallucinations in that they occur during the course of intense religious experience rather than during a psychotic episode...Visions are, then, special kinds of dreams". He proposes an important and original view of visions as transient reactions lessening the agony of separation. The guru-disciple relationship is shown to be much like the mother-child attachment, and much like certain forms of modern psychotherapy. Some of the examples are taken from contemporary religious movements, where the data are relevant to our attempts to understand the concept of "charisma".

913. Hitschmann, E. Swedenborg's paranoia. *American Imago*, 1949, *6*, 45-50.

Swedenborg is presented quite convincingly as a successful Dr. Schreber, and Schreber as a failed Swedenborg. In the former case, paranoid delusions became the established doctrine of religious movement, read and followed by tens of thousands. The dynamics in both cases was the same: regression from sublimated homosexuality to narcissistic paranoia. Swedenborg succeeded where Schreber failed because, apparently, his narcissism still allowed for considerable contact with reality. This is an interesting and important contribution to understanding the personalities of founders in religious movements.

914. Kligerman, C. A psychoanalytic study of the confessions of St. Augustine. *Journal of the American Psychoanalytic Association*, 1957, *5*, 469-484.

This is a true model of psychoanalytic interpretation, clear and eloquent, aided no doubt by the compelling nature of the material. *The Confessions* are so filled with evidence for psychoanalytic hypotheses, from early Oedipal rivalry to the dynamics of Oedipal conversion, that the analyst just has to pick up ready-made pieces. It is small wonder that so many psychoanalytic interpretations have followed this one.

915. Lubin, A.J. Vincent van Gogh's ear. *Psychoanalytic Quarterly*, 1961, *30*, 351-384.

Van Gogh's self-mutilation, which was overdetermined, did also have some religious meanings. He was strongly affected by Christianity, identified with Jesus, and projected on others the traditions regarding other New Testament figures. Lubin speculates that the body of Jesus, and that the prostitute Rachel, who received it, represented both Mary the virgin mother and Mary Magdalene.

916. Moxon, C. Epileptic traits in Paul of Tarsus. *Psychoanalytic Review*, 1922, *9*, 60-66.

On the basis of writings attributed to Paul in the New Testament, the author goes beyond religious doctrines and attempts a personality analysis. The reader must remain skeptical, as the personality involved has been glimpsed only very indirectly. This is indeed long-distance diagnosis, not only over space but also over time!

917. Ohayon, S.I. In search of Akhnaton. *American Imago*, 1982, *39*, 165-179.

Combining meager historical evidence with much speculation, this article asserts that Akhnaton suffered from paranoia, and relates this to evidence about his homosexual tendencies.

918. Saffady, E. The effects of childhood bereavement and parental remarriage in Sixteenth century England: The case of Thomas More. *History of Childhood Quarterly*, 1973, *1*, 310-336.

Early childhood traumas are used to explain the beliefs and the eventual martyrdom of Sir Thomas More. The problem is how to account for the exceptional qualities of the person, beyond the common and inevitable crises that befall all of us.

919. Smith, P. Luther's early development in the light of psychoanalysis. *American Journal of Psychology*, 1913, *24*, 360-377.

This early attempt at psychobiography is remarkable for its success in gathering information from the public record. Based on many autobiographical statements by Luther, and some testimonies of contemporaries, the author concludes that his subject was "... a thoroughly typical example of the neurotic, quasi-hysterical sequence of an infantile sex-complex". His obsession with the Devil, sexuality, incest, and anality are discussed. It is clear that Luther was able to overcome the disabling effects of these obsessions through a remarkable conversion which made him into an effective historical leader.

920. Strachey, J. Preliminary notes upon the problem of Akhnaten. *International Journal of Psychoanalysis*, 1939, *20*, 33-42.

This is a speculative article, suggesting that the ancient Egyptian king, who supposedly created monotheism had a an "unusually large feminine component" in his personality. The combination of his feminine tendencies with his position as the omnipotent ruler of Egypt led to the appearance of monotheism. Naturally, there is little evidence for this speculation, but the hypothesis about femininity and monotheism may be worth pursuing.

921. Woollcott, P. Some considerations of creativity and religious experience in St. Augustine of Hippo. *Journal for the Scientific Study of Religion*, 1966, *5*, 273-283.

This is a thorough analysis of Augustine's (auto)biography, seeing it as dominated by Oedipal problems. Augustine's conversion is typical, and God represents the father. Giving up sexuality means final submission to paternal authority. It leads to creativity and happiness because of the peace between ego and superego forces, which saves psychic energy that formerly was invested in their conflict. This is a lucid and important contribution.

922. Yarom, N. *Body, Blood and Sexuality*. New York: Peter Lang, 1992.

This is a psychoanalytic biography of St. Francis of Assisi, informed by the literature on hysteria and stigmata. Francesco Bernardona, the future St. Francis, is described as suffering from an unresolved Oedipal problem, which led him to refuse the social and sexual roles expected of a man, thus causing a severe crisis at age 25. In addition, Francesco had an effeminate, passive-homosexual component in his personality. The inability to identify with his real father led him to identify with Jesus as a substitute. His passive-homosexual role could be well fulfilled in his religious vocation as an apostle of love. It is suggested that the psychic development of St. Francis was very similar to that of Freud's famous analysand, known as the Wolfman. The physical symptom of the stigmata, which St. Francis was the first to have, is the focus of an analysis of its symbolic meaning and its value as a way of unconscious need gratification. The stigmata are interpreted as a form of self-sacrifice and self-castration. The collective crisis experienced by Francesco's society, paralleling the individual one, is delineated.

For additional materials on this topic, see also 224, 613, 809, 810, 813, 821, 1520, 1603.

10

MYTHOLOGY

1001.   Arlow, J.A. Ego psychology and the study of mythology. *Journal of the American Psychoanalytic Association*, 1961, *9*, 371-393.

The capacity for mythmaking is discussed from the point of view of psychoanalytic structural theory. Myths, together with dreams, fantasies, and symptoms, stem from the instinctual conflicts of childhood. Myths relieve guilt and anxiety, constitute a form of adaptation to reality, and affect identity and superego formation. Mythmaking creates a common, socializing experience, which is acted out through ritual and drama. These communal experiences support the ego in his struggles against id and superego.

1002.   Balter, L. The mother as a source of power: A psychoanalytic study of three Greek myths. *Psychoanalytic Quarterly*, 1969, *38*, 217-274.

The one important and original claim here is that myths reflect both early childhood experiences and cultural, historical values. In the examples given here, those reflect the struggle between matriarchy and patriarchy.

1003.   Barnouw, V. A psychological interpretation of a Chippewa origin legend. *Journal of American Folklore*, 1955, *68*, 73-85, 211-223, 341-355.

This work is inspired by the "culture and personality" school, which assumes that common patterns of child-rearing in a given culture will lead to a common basic personality structure. The common personality will be marked by particular emphases on genital and pre-genital themes, following early childhood experiences in particular psychosexual stages. In this particular cultural example, mythology is treated as a projection of these defense patterns which are both individual and cultural. The prominence of pre-genital themes in Chippewa mythology reflects early frustration in the oral and anal stages. One problem with this analysis is that these legends may be found in other native cultures of North America, and are not unique to the Chippewa (see 1018 below).

1004. Beck, S.J. Cosmic optimism in some Genesis myths. *American Journal of Orthopsychiatry*, 1971, *41*, 380-389.

Following Harry Stack Sullivan, Beck suggests that myths express strongly felt inner needs, like dreams or schizophrenic language. The early chapters of the book of Genesis are the products of a mythmaker that invented a good God and created him in man's image. Then the good God has become an introject, enabling humans to cope with the human condition.

1005. Berger, J. New views of the Biblical Joseph. *American Journal of Psychoanalysis*, 1981, *41*, 277-282.

The author is impressed with Joseph's reported dream interpretations, which seem to him totally psychoanalytic. However, it is totally unclear who was the dreamer, and who was the interpreter, and where the whole story belongs.

1006. Bergmann, M.S. The impact of ego psychology on the study of the myth. *American Imago*, 1966, *23*, 257-264.

This is a summary of several presentation in a 1962 panel on the subject and reviews several suggestions regarding ego and superego functions of myths.

1007. Bonaparte, M. Saint Christopher patron saint of the motor car drivers. *American Imago*, 1947, *4*, 49-77.

The Christian Saint Christopher is found, on closer examination, to be a reincarnation of the Egyptian jackal-headed god, Anubis, the bearer of the dead. Like other deities from the pagan pantheon, Anubis has been adopted by Christianity.

1008. Boyer, L.B. Stone as a symbol in Apache mythology. *American Imago*, 1965, *22*, 14-39.

Variations in Apache myths were interpreted as helping group members to deal with oral dependency, oral sadism, Oedipal problems, and sibling rivalry, through partial repression. Their particular forms are said to reflect Apache socialization, characterized as phallic-oral-sadistic, resulting in a typical personality marked by typical conflicts.

1009. Boyer, L.B. and Boyer, R.M. A combined anthropological and psychoanalytic contribution to folklore. *Psychopathologie Africaine*, 1967, *3*, 333-372.

Variations in the telling of a legend dealing with supernatural forces and personal transformations are analyzed as reflecting both unconscious individual conflicts and objective social conditions. Shared fantasies are viewed as originating in early experiences, such as sibling rivalry. The authors asked several informants to tell the same story, and this is an example of an innovating technique in psychoanalytic anthropology.

1010.   Bradley, N. Primal scene experience in human evolution and its phantasy derivatives in art, proto-science and philosophy.   *The Psychoanalytic Study of Society*, 1967, *4*, 34-79.

Primal scene experiences are considered a severe ontogenetic trauma, which has left its mark on all human cultures. Such experiences are naturally more common in traditional and poorer cultures, where crowded living conditions and lack of privacy are a fact of life. Evidence for displaced primal scene experiences are found in a variety of cultural products, including creation myths, from the Stone Age through the Middle Ages to our time.

1011.   Bunker, A.H. The feast of Tantalus. *Psychoanalytic Quarterly*, 1952, *21*, 355-372.

This myth is interpreted as expressing a puberty initiation process, in which the all powerful father grants the initiate adult status and prerogatives in return for giving up ties to the mother.

1012.   Bunker, A.H. Tantalus: A preoedipal figure of myth. *Psychoanalytic Quarterly*, 1953, *22*, 159-173.

Various sins are attributed to Tantalus in Greek mythology. According to one tradition, he tempted the gods, by serving them at a banquet the flesh of his own son Pelops, to see it they could tell that it was human. This is compared to the sins of Prometheus and Sisyphus, all involved in exposing divine secrets. All three suffer oral punishment, because their sins of unlimited appetite were also oral.

1013.   Caldwell, R. *The Origin of the Gods*. New York: Oxford University Press, 1989.

This study by a classicist of Greek theogonic myths starts with the assumption that myth allows the expression of unconscious ideas in socially acceptable forms. Other goals, cognitive in nature, may also be served, by they are energized by childhood concerns This is illustrated by the stories about the relations between Gaia, Rhea, and Zeus. This is an important contribution that should serve as a model for further work not only on myth, but on religion in general.

1014.   Campbell, J. Bios and Mythos: Prolegomena to a science of mythology. In N. Wilbur and W. Muensterberger (eds.) *Psychoanalysis and Culture*. New York: International Universities Press, 1981.

This general statement on the history of research in mythology starts with the finding that certain beliefs, which form the basis of mythological preoccupations, are universal or "...about coterminous with the human species". They include the belief in immortality, the belief in the efficacy of ritual and magic, the belief in a sacred power, and the belief in the relationship of dream and mythology. The possibility for real research on these phenomena was created by the appearance of *Totem and Taboo*. In addition to Freud, Roheim is credited with having made the most important contributions to the understanding of culture and mythology.

1015.   Cox. H.L. The place of mythology in the study of culture. *American Imago*, 1948, 5, 83-94.

Mythology is a reflection of any given culture's anxieties and its typical early childhood experiences. This hypothesis is tested in the case of the South Pacific Marquesan culture. It turns out that the subjects which appear more commonly in its legends are food, sex, and hostility towards women, which might have been predicted.

1016.   de Monchy, S.J.R. Adam-Cain-Oedipus. *American Imago*, 1962, *19*, 3-17.

The Cain-Abel myth is treated as a dream, and the two brothers are interpreted as two aspects of the same personality, one father-hating and the other father-loving. The rebellious self had to destroy the obedient self before going out into the world, creating a family and then a nation skilled in crafts.

1017.   Deutsch, H. *A Psychoanalytic Study of the Myth of Dionysus and Apollo*. New York: International Universities Press, 1969.

This slim volume contains much in the way of both data and interpretation. The two Greek gods are viewed as reflecting two patterns of mother-son relationship. Dionysus is marked by his bisexuality and his struggle for immortality, and is led to saving his mother. Apollo, marked by male-female duality, is led to killing his own mother. This work is exemplary, as strands of mythological are woven together to form of unique collage of individual and cultural motives.

1018.   Dundes, A. Earth diver: Creation of the mythopoeic male. *American Anthropologist*, 1962, *64*, 1032-1051.

This is a general presentation of, and a defense of, the psychoanalytic approach to mythology, which also contains one specific case study. The myth of the earth-diver, telling the story of a little tiny bit of mud with which the world has been created, is interpreted as expressing the fantasy of anal creation and procreation. It is based on 2 assumptions: 1. the prevalence of a cloacal theory of birth, and 2. the existence of pregnancy envy in males.

1019.   Dundes, A. The flood: A male myth of creation. *Journal of Psychoanalytic Anthropology*, 1986, *9*, 359-372.

The numerous flood stories found in countless mythologies around the world tell always of a male who destroys the world and then another male who recreates humanity after the disaster. These stories are expressions of male envy of females because of their ability to procreate. A similar myth is that of the creation of woman from a male's rib or other body parts, commonly found in various traditions. This is an original, important contribution.

1020.   Edelheit, H. Mythopoesis and the primal scene. *Psychoanalytic Study of Society*, 1972, *5*, 212-233.

Suggests that all children possess a primal scene schema, which antedates the Oedipal configuration and determines the latter's form. Claims that primal scene experiences and primal scene fantasies play a major role in the demonology and mythology of most cultures. This claim is illustrated with numerous examples from art, literature, and film.

1021.   Fingert, H.H. Psychoanalytic study of the minor prophet, Jonah. *The Psychoanalytic Review*, 1954, *41*, 55-65.

This is a speculative interpretation, based on the notion that the Biblical text represents an "... allegorical form of an emotional disturbance in which a religious delusional fantasy occurred". The famous storm at sea is viewed as a childhood memory of the primal scene, or a projection of Jonah's own (stormy) sexual impulses. Being swallowed by the fish is a return to the womb, etc. The final product reflects much psychoanalytic creativity, as long as it is judged to be solely a textual exegesis.

1022.   Fodor, A. The fall of man in the book of Genesis. *American Imago*, 1954, *11*, 201-231.

This far ranging discussion of ancient mythology in West Asia regards the story of Eden as a sublimated and sanitized version of earlier polytheistic traditions. God in the story is a representation of primal father, with Eve being his consort. She might have assumed once the form of a serpent, thus being a phallic woman. Her separation from the penis (represented by Adam's loss of a rib) introduced the character of Adam. Eve is degraded by becoming Adam's consort, and the serpent is cursed as well, symbolizing the decline and fall of the Mother Goddess. The betrayal of the Great Mother is the Original Sin, a source of eternal guilt. The analysis here is informed by both ancient mythology and psychoanalytic hypotheses about early childhood experiences of the parents, to create a stimulating combination.

1023.   Fortune, R.F. The symbolism of the serpent. *International Journal of Psychoanalysis*, 1926, *7*, 237-243.

To determine the symbolic meaning of the serpent in the Garden of Eden story, Fortune draws on a similar myth, found among the Maoris. In that version of the creation myth, woman is created by man, and then appears an eel to stimulate the woman sexually and spoil Paradise. The clear sexual significance of the eel in the Maori version is viewed as supporting an interpretation of the "original sin" as involving carnal knowledge. This is an interesting and original exercise in the use of anthropological data.

1024.   Goldfrank, E.S. "Old Man" and the father image in Blood (Blackfoot) society. In G.B. Wilbur and W. Muensterberger (eds.) *Psychoanalysis and Culture*. New York: International Universities Press, 1951.

Objective historical and economic changes in the conditions of one native American group, in addition to changes in family relations, have led to corresponding modifications of the image of the father in myth. Originally described as a generous creator, the father's image has deteriorated so that it now more often appears as a malevolent prankster. This newer negative image allows expression of the son's hostility towards his father, in a society where stated norms calls for the latter's idealization. This is a striking example of cultural projection mechanisms.

1025. Goldman, H.E. Paradise destroyed: The crime of being born: A psychoanalytic study of the experience of evil. *Contemporary Psychoanalysis*, 1988, *24*, 420-450.

This interesting article contains an interpretation of the Genesis story of the Fall, which suggests that the perception of one's own birth as destruction of a parental paradise leads to guilt feelings. Children of narcissistically damaged parents can feel guilty about being alive, as if their birth had disrupted a paradise between their parents. The feeling of guilt derives from projective identification by the parents.

1026. Gonen, J.Y. Then men said: "Let us make God in our image, after our likeness". *Literature and Psychology*, 1971, *21*, 69-79.

The Genesis Garden of Eden myth is interpreted and God's image is analyzed as a truly human projection. God is both humanity in its reality, as well as humanity's ideal self. Therefore he is far from omnipotent or perfect. The story reflects also a dual deity, which is part of Judaic traditions.

1027. Graber, R.B. The trials of passio domini: A footnote to the psychoanalysis of Christianity. *Journal of Psychoanalytic Anthropology*, 1986, *9*, 35-40.

Following suggestions that the crucifixion in Christian mythology is a symbolic castration, the author draws attention to the connection between the crucifixion story and the number three, which appears often in the New Testament, and represents the male genitals.

1028. Grinstein, A. Stages in the development of control over fire. *International Journal of Psychoanalysis*, 1952, *33*, 416-420.

Myths of the origin of fire, most commonly stolen from the gods, males and females, are interpreted as reflecting actual pre-historical stages in gaining control over fire, as well as ego-developmental stages. The projection in myth is then both of dramatic reality and dramatic internal experiences.

1029. Groot, A.D. de, *Saint Nicholas: A Psychoanalytic Study of His History and Myth.* The Hague: Mouton, 1965.

This is a meticulous and scholarly survey of many legends and works of arts, reflecting the Medieval traditions regarding St. Nicholas. The interpretation of these materials is of unusual depth and seriousness. The author raises general questions regarding the validity of psychoanalytic interpretations, but concludes by supporting Freud's classical notions of dream interpretations. While the latent aspect is understood to reflect basic infantile (and adult) concerns about sex, birth, and the family, the manifest level is adopted, and St. Nick is recognized as bearing the gift of human love (see 1134).

1030.   Hofling, C.E. Notes on Raychaudhuri's "Jesus Christ and Sir Krisna". *American Imago*, 1958, *15*, 213-226.

This is a classical critique of the uncritical use of mythology as biographical fact. The only problem is that Hofling's critique itself is guilty of the same sin, accepting Christian scriptures as reliable sources.

1031.   Huckel, H. The tragic guilt of Prometheus. *American Imago*, 1955, *12*, 325-336.

The story of Prometheus has been told and interpreted many times. Here is a commendable attempt at integrating literary and psychoanalytic traditions, with reference to clinical material. Prometheus' fateful deed was a rebellion against father, and thus he is an Oedipal child. At the same time, he is the pioneer of human sublimation and culture, and thus a precursor of the superego. The son eventually prevails over his father, as all sons can. Many sons experience conflict when their own development is experienced as an unconscious threat to their fathers. The myth is found to be humanistic and heroic.

1032.   Jones, E. The Madonna's Conception through the ear -- a contribution to the relation between aesthetics and religion (1914). In E. Jones, *Essays in Applied Psychoanalysis*. Vol. 2. London: The Hogarth Press and the Institute of Psychoanalysis, 1951.

This legend, pictorially represented in medieval and Renaissance art, is interpreted as a sublimated version of various infantile fantasies, which deny the father any generative powers through a focus on anality. The conscious idea is that of the least sensual form of procreation. Its unconscious counterpart is the complete opposite, totally repellent to the adult mind.

1033.   Jones, E. A psychoanalytic study of the Holy Ghost concept (1922). In E. Jones *Essays in Applied Psychoanalysis*. Vol. 2. The Hogarth Press and the Institute of Psychoanalysis, London, 1951.

This insightful essay contains a number of important hypotheses regarding the origins, and consequences, of Christian myths. The idea of the Holy Ghost in Christian mythology is a solution to a conflict about the image of the Mother Goddess. When the Mother Goddess is replaced in certain Christian traditions by the image of the Holy Ghost, this reflected a transition from incestuous and parricidal desires to a stronger attachment to the father. The Great Mother Goddess is thus split into two: Mary the Mother of God and the Holy Ghost. The Holy Ghost occupies the original place of the Great Goddess in the Trinity. This "Ghost" is endowed with paternal generative power, which means that it represents the phallic mother. Mariolatry is tied to "self-castration" and homosexual passivity, as shown by the garb and lifestyle of Catholic priests. The Protestant Reformation represents a return to the Jewish position by rejecting Mariolatry.

1034. Kaplan, B. Psychological themes in Zuni mythology and Zuni TAT's. *Psychoanalytic Study of Society*, 1962, *2*, 255-262.

This research report tried to correlate themes in mythology and personal themes as expressed on a projective test. The finding was that there was a clear gap between the myth level and the personality level. This should make us cautious before we attempt to generalize from the collective dreams of mythology to individual dreamers and their personal myths.

1035. Kluckhohn, C. Myths and rituals: a general theory. *Harvard Theological Review*, 1942, *35*, 45-79.

This general theory adopts the view that neither myth nor ritual are primary. Both are cultural responses to anxiety. Ritual is a repetitive action in response to threat, while the myth rationalizes it. Both provide sublimation and security for the ego.

1036. Kluckhohn, C. Recurrent themes in myths and myth-making. *Daedalus*, 1959, *88*, 268-279.

This is an important statement by a leading student of culture and cultures. The following themes are found to appear in numerous mythologies around the world: creation, flood, slaying of monsters, incest, sibling rivalry, castration (and vagina dentata), Oedipal stories, and hero myths. These recurrent themes in myths are said to "... result from recurrent reactions of the human psyche to situations and stimuli of the same general order". This fits with Freud's notion of the psychic unity of mankind and the universality of early experiences, represented in dreams and symbols.

1037. Lederer, W. Historical consequences of father-son hostility. *Psychoanalytic Review*, 1967, *54*, 248-276.

This is a speculative, far-reaching article on a universal theme. Collective consciousness, in the form of both religious and secular mythologies, reflects awareness of the dangerous consequences of father-son hostility. This conflict is not only celebrated, but also controlled, by society and cultural traditions.

1038. Lederer, W. Oedipus and the serpent. *Psychoanalytic Review*, 1964-65, *51*, 619-644.

Various versions of the common creation myth are investigated for references to the Garden and the serpent in it. The serpent in the myth of the Garden of Eden is interpreted as a rebelling serpent-god about to usurp the throne of the serpent-father Jahweh. References to the serpent, compared to Jesus, are found in the New Testament, and the cross is referred to as the "tree of life".

1039. Levin, A.J. Oedipus and Samson, the rejected hero-child. *International Journal of Psychoanalysis*, 1957, *38*, 105-116.

Suggests that the myths of Samson and Oedipus are historically and psychodynamically related. Samson's upbringing is considered to have been one of abandonment and exposure, deprived of normal mothering. In both stories a monster is destroyed and riddles are involved, and both heroes lost their eyesight. Early exposure myths are aimed at justifying the cruelty of ancient child-rearing traditions. One problem with this article is that it confuses mythological figures with historical persons.

1040. Lowenfeld, H. Freud's Moses and Bismarck. *Psychoanalysis and the Social Sciences*, 1950, *2*, 277

Wild speculation about Bismarck's role as a father figure in German history, with guilt feelings etc., inspired by Freud's wild speculations about the Jewish people's feelings about Moses.

1041. Marcus, N.N. Prometheus reconsidered. *Psychoanalytic Review*, 1967, *54*, 83-107.

An interesting application of ego-psychology to mythology. The resolution of the conflict between Zeus and Prometheus is presented as a reality-principle compromise. Both curb their id urges when their limitations are realized.

1042. Medlicott, R.W. The case of Joseph: The strengths and hazards of narcissistic omnipotence. *British Journal of Medical Psychology*, 1980, *53*, 187-190.

Treats the mythological Joseph as a real personality, and ascribes to him paranoid megalomania, among other things. This is a parody of psychoanalytic interpretation.

1043. Merkur, D. Adaptive symbolism and the theory of myth: The symbolic understanding of myth in Inuit religion. *The Psychoanalytic Study of Society*, 1988, *13*, 63-94.

The author proposes a system of myth-analysis and a definition of myth. Myths are narratives believed to be true, whose characters include supernatural figures, and report on the divinities' powers and activities. They symbolize abstract ideas and serve as "charters" to religious rites and institutions. Myth analysis, following the work of Roheim and Rank, and based on psychoanalytic dream-interpretation, reconstructs the religious ideas expressed through them.

1044. Moloney, J.C. Carnal myths involving the sun. *American Imago*, 1963, *20*, 93-104

Sunrise and sunset are complete mysteries to humans deprived of modern sciences. Myths that arise in response to them often describe the sun as being swallowed, eliminated, or breaking out of the body. Such stories reflect mainly oral anxieties and drives, as well as other infantile fantasies about childbirth and sexuality.

1045.   More, J. The prophet Jonah: The story of an intrapsychic process. *American Imago*, 1970, *27*, 3-11.

Offers an interpretation of the second part of the Biblical book of Jonah, regarded as similar to a psychotherapeutic dialogue. It is unclear where this intrapsychic dialogue has taken place.

1046.   Muensterberger, W. Remarks on the function of mythology. *The Psychoanalytic Study of Society*, 1964, *3*, 94-97.

This important theoretical contribution suggests that to understand the psychosocial role of religious beliefs and practices, we have to combine ego psychology with the study of environmental conditions and cultural changes. Mythology tests out hypotheses about all existing id impulses and all possible object relations.

1047.   Niederland, W.G. Jacob's dream: with some remarks on ladder and river symbolism. *Journal of the Hillside Hospital*, 1954, *3*, 73-97.

Jacob's dream, described in the Book of Genesis, is interpreted as a fantasy of an Oedipal triumph over the father. The dreamer is treated as a real person and a real personality. The author engages in some dubious interpretations of Hebrew words, and in calculations based on the numerical value of Hebrew letters (a Talmudic tradition, which is here misinterpreted). The article deteriorates into a caricature of psychoanalytic interpretation.

1048.   Obeyesekere, G. *The Work of Culture: Symbolic Transformation In Psychoanalysis and Anthropology*. Chicago: The University of Chicago Press, 1991.

This important book contains many significant examples of Hindu and Buddhist myths and rituals, interpreted in a classical psychoanalytic way, even though it is claimed that a simple Oedipal model does not fit the products of all human cultures.

1049.   Petrus, E.P. The Golem: Significance of the legend. *The Psychoanalytic Review*, 1966, *53*, 63-68.

The late medieval Jewish legend of the Golem of Prague, a powerful creature who was supposedly formed by a famous rabbi, is interpreted as reflecting a flight into fantasy, and a repetition-compulsion mechanism.

1050.   Pruyser, P.W. and Luke, J.T. The epic of Gilgamesh. *American Imago*, 1982, *39*, 73-93.

This ancient epic is interpreted as reflecting stages of personality development throughout the life cycle, following a model which combines classical psychoanalysis with the Erikson model. The hero's progress starts with a narcissistic-phallic phase, through an Oedipal crisis, latency, identity, and generativity.

1051.   Rank, O. *The Myth of the Birth of the Hero: A Psychological Interpretation of Mythology*. Nervous and Mental Diseases Monograph Series 18, New York:

Nervous and Mental Diseases Publishing Co. 1914. (originally published in 1909, with numerous reprints of the English version since 1914).

This is the classical foundation of the psychoanalytic study of mythology, which has lost none of its punch over the years. After looking at 34 myths from the Mediterranean basin and West Asia, Rank offers a general formula, a "standard saga", which can be found in innumerable mythological stories. The mythological hero is presented as the son of royal parents, born of a difficult birth (often after a long period of childlessness), prophesied to be a danger to the safety of his father, who banishes him (often by putting him in a basket and setting it afloat). The child is saved by poor people or animals, and only upon maturity does he discover his real parents, following numerous adventures. He eventually gains the love and recognition of his people, achieves fame and greatness, and wreaks vengeance on his father, in accordance with the prophecy.

This formula fits the well known myths of Moses, Isaac, Oedipus, and Jesus. [This general model was expanded by Raglan in *The Hero: a Study in Tradition, Myth, and Drama*. London: Methuen, 1936]. But Rank's contribution is not in discovering the general formula, but in offering a psychoanalytic interpretation in terms of early childhood experiences. It is the family romance of neurotics, common to all cultures, which is the root of this myth pattern. In this fantasy, the child gets rid of his parents and is adopted by others of much higher status. In a later version only the father is replaced. The hostility towards the father is projected on him in the myth, where the child is always the victim.

1052.   Reider, N. Chess, Oedipus and the Mater Dolorosa. *International Journal of Psychoanalysis*, 1959, *40*, 515-528.

In a discussion of the unconscious meaning of chess, this article reviews many ancient West Asian myths as well as Christian mythology, and suggests that while many pre-Oedipal elements can be found in legends about Mary and Jesus, it is the Oedipal themes which predominate.

1053.   Reider, N. Medieval Oedipal legends about Judas. *Psychoanalytic Quarterly*, 1960, *29*, 515-527.

Based on the most comprehensive sources, this article surveys the medieval phenomenon of legends about the New Testament figure of Judas, which follow closely the original Oedipus myth, and a parallel Jewish legend. The story apparently appeared in Europe in the 11th century, and it is suggested that the Crusades and anti-Semitism played a role in its popularity, as well as heightened concern about incest taboos. The Oedipal legend about Judas is analyzed as a parallel to the Oedipal Jesus myth. It is pointed out that the mother-son mythological tradition may be viewed as pre-Oedipal, as well as Oedipal.

1054.   Reik, T. *Myth and Guilt: The Crime and Punishment of Mankind*. New York: Braziller, 1957.

This typical Reikian chef d'oeuvre deals with two myths: the Fall of Adam and the crucifixion of Jesus. The starting point is a refusal to accept standard interpretation of the Fall and Original Sin, which allude to a primordial sexual offense. Moreover, Reik points out correctly that the Original Sin doctrine started with Christianity's claims of its atonement through the Crucifixion. In sayings attributed to Christ himself, Original Sin is never mentioned. The Fall story itself appears in numerous versions all over the world, but Reik searches for the core myth. Its reconstruction leads to the following conclusion: The Original Sin was killing and devouring God, which was expressed in the language of tree totemism. This mythological crime was atoned for by the mythological Crucifixion. The Christian Eucharist is a re-enactment of this cannibalistic crime and punishment. This is a very personal, clever and speculative work of psychoanalytic archeology.

1055.　Reik, T. *Mystery of the Mountain: The Drama of the Sinai Revelation.* New York: Harper, 1959.

This is the most speculative of Reik's exercises in psychoanalytic archeology. While accepting the myth of the exodus from Egypt as history, Reik regards the story of the revelation on Mount Sinai as a reflection of an ancient initiation ritual. But this time the initiation was directed at the whole people of Israel. A more interesting idea is of the similarity (or the identity) between the Jesus myth and puberty rites.

1056.　Reik, T. *The Creation of Woman: A Psychoanalytic Inquiry into the Myth of Eve.* New York: Braziller, 1960.

Reik is engaged in "archeological psychoanalysis", and following his long-held conception, views the Eve myth as another reflection of ancient Semitic puberty rites, in which young boys had to (symbolically) experience death and rebirth. The removal of Adam's rib has to do with ritual mutilations (like circumcision), characterizing most initiation traditions. The final possession of a woman is the common outcome of male initiation.

1057.　Reik, T. *The Temptation.* New York: Braziller, 1961.

The Biblical story of the offering of Isaac is interpreted, following Reik's by now familiar theory, as reflecting pre-historical puberty initiation traditions. These initiation rites included circumcision, and dramatic enactments of death and rebirth. The myth depicts Isaac, the cult hero, as being attacked by a demon god who demands human sacrifice. Thus, the myth preserves the memory of an ancient son-god, a rebel who was eventually defeated. The familiar Old Testament version of the story, while reflecting stone-age traditions, may also show signs of Judaic struggles against human sacrifice. This is possibly the clearest exposition of Reik's initiation rite thesis.

1058.　Roheim, G. The Garden of Eden. *Psychoanalytic Review,* 1940, *27,* 1-26; 177-199.

After surveying many similar myths from around the world, all dealing with creation, sin and mortality, Roheim first offers an Oedipal interpretation of the Eden myth. Adam's sin is in rebelling against the omnipotent father and his consummated desire for Eve, the mother. The original sin is followed by the first experience of guilt and the development of the superego. Sexual desire is disobedience to the father, and a sin to the invisible "voice" heard in Eden, the introjected father imago (superego).

A second, pre-Oedipal interpretation of the myth then focuses on the oral stage and the baby's early oral aggression towards the mother. While the tree of life is the father's, or God's, penis, it also symbolizes the mother. The apples of immortality are the mother's breasts and nipples, but ambivalence exists already during the oral stage, and the baby wishes to destroy the mother's body. Separation from the mother is the primal trauma, the banishment from Eden, where all want to return.

1059.   Roheim, G. Myth and folk tale. *American Imago*, 1941, *2*, 266-279.

This is an important theoretical statements about two kinds of traditional narratives. While myths are part of a creedal system, and relate the action of divine beings, folk tales describe the actions of mere mortals. But both have a common origin: Oedipal conflicts.

1060.   Roheim, G. The panic of the gods. *Psychoanalytic Quarterly*, 1952, *21*, 92-106.

The universal theme of the gods in panic is analyzed and its developmental origins are suggested. In these myths the gods are terrified because of the approach of a monster or a demon, and the monster is frightened away by the strongest male god, with the help of what seems like a phallus. An example from Babylonian mythology describes Tiamat, the chaos goddess who is about to destroy the gods, who is defeated by Marduk. This is interpreted as based on an early childhood nightmare, in which anxieties over oral-aggressive wishes are overcome by a shift to genital wishes.

1061.   Seidenberg, R. Sacrificing the first you see. *The Psychoanalytic Review*, 1966, *53*, 49-62.

The vow to kill the first one you see (usually a daughter) on coming home from war is a legendary theme found in ancient Hebrew and Greek mythology. It is interpreted as an assault against the first internalized object, i.e. the mother. It is also a way of reconciling with the father (or father-god) and of renouncing femininity.

1062.   Slochower, H. Psychoanalytic distinction between myth and mythopoesis. *Journal of the American Psychoanalytic Association*, 1970, *18*, 150-164.

Mythopoesis does not only explain the world and preserve the social order. It may also strive to change them, through mythological heroes in rebellion against reality. While myths provide the group with its collective identity, they may also foster individual identity through identification.

1063.   Slochower, H. *Mythopoesis*. Detroit: Wayne State University Press, 1970.

Mythopoesis (from the Greek *poiein*, to create) introduces an ego element, through an individual artist who re-creates old legends. Examples are *Hamlet, Faust*, the book of Job, Greek tragedies. The mythopoeic accounts appear when literal accounts of the legend can no longer be accepted. The artist's recreation promotes rebellion and change, as the individual creative artist expresses his ego, as well as his individualized superego. While mythology expresses a defense against instinctual drives, mythopoesis encourages individual autonomy and collective change. It is a meeting point between the mythical hero and his real followers, who may be inspired to great creativity and even revolutionary upheavals.

1064.   Spiro, M.E. Virgin birth, parthenogenesis, and physiological paternity: An essay in cultural interpretation. *Man*, 1968, *3*, 242-261.

As part of a debate over beliefs in paternity in Trobriand culture, Spiro looks at 2 cases: the belief in a spirit-child which enters the womb, thus causing pregnancy, and the Christian belief in the Virgin Birth. Both are attempts at Oedipal (re)solution, in which individual fantasy turns into cultural structures. Like all works by Spiro, this is a seminal contribution.

1065.   Sterba, R. A Dutch celebration of a festival. *American Imago*, 1941, *2*, 205-208.

The Christian tradition has unconsciously connected the myths of St. Stephen, the slaughter of the Innocents, and the birth of Jesus. The connection is that all the heroes of these myths were engaged in a rebellion against a father-figure, and were punished by death. This is tied to an Oedipal interpretation of the myth of Jesus.

1066.   Sterba, R. On Hallowe'en. *American Imago*, 1948, *5*, 213-224.

Contrasts the attitudes towards death in European and United States culture, and concludes that the American attitude is characterized by denial. In Europe the dead are remembered through collective rituals and their graves attended on All Souls Day. In the United States, the popular observance of Hallowe'en, carried out by children, represents the "return of the repressed" in this case. The dead, neglected by adults, return as children wearing frightening masks. In this way the children are also unconsciously offered as sacrifice to the dead. These speculations have to be weighed more carefully against evidence about similar practices in other cultures.

1067.   Stern, M. Ego psychology, myth and rite: Remarks about the relationship of the individual and the group. *The Psychoanalytic Study of Society*, 1964, *3*, 71-93.

This is an important statement along the lines of ego-psychology. It suggests that myth and ritual are not only ways of discharging repressed instinctual drives. The narcissistic sexualized thinking which characterizes them results from both objective conditions of life in earlier times, and subjective dependency feelings of humans. The ego aspect of myth and ritual is found in the mastery of danger through magic, which liberates the ego for reality testing. The myth is a verbalization of fantasies which accompany the magical act. Myths and rituals support both individual and collective identity. Ecstasy rituals represent a fantasy regression to the mother-child symbiosis.

1068. Theodoropoulus, J. "Adam's Rib". *The Psychoanalytic Review*, 1967, *54*, 150-152.

The choice of Adam's rib as the origin of Eve in Biblical mythology is interpreted as representing male fantasies about penile erection. The male organ, experienced as having a bone inside it, is indeed responsible for procreation. This myth, denying the female role in procreation, is also viewed as belonging to the "devouring female" theme, as the rib-penis disappears inside her.

1069. Trevett, L.D. Origin of the creation myth: a hypothesis. *Journal of the American Psychoanalytic Association*, 1957, *5*, 461-468.

It is suggested that the creation myth in the book of Genesis is an expression of the earliest perceptions of the infant. It moves from the recognition of the breast to the recognition of person through stages of differentiation, from chaos to an orderly world. The tendency to recapture the infant's early perceptions is found in individuals as well.

1070. Watkins, J.G. Concerning Freud's paper on "The Moses of Michaelangelo". *American Imago*, 1951, *8*, 61-63.

Suggests that in Michaelangelo's rendering, Moses does not break the tablets, and thus does not assume a castrating posture vis-à-vis his followers. This should explain viewers' responses to this work of art.

1071. Weiss, S.A. The biblical story of Ruth: Analytic implications of the Hebrew masoretic text. *American Imago*, 1959, *16*, 195-209.

The story of Ruth is analyzed as a literary work, with the help of traditional notations found in the Biblical text, which are interpreted as revealing unconscious motivations.

1072. Wittels, F. Psychoanalysis and history: The Nibelungs and the Bible. *The Psychoanalytic Quarterly*, 1946, *15*, 88-103.

A speculative attempt to deal with "collective psychology" through myths considered representative of national groups. The Song of the Nibelungs is considered to represent the pagan, immature German spirit. The Bible represents Judaism and Christianity, rejected by the Germans. Paradoxically, Biblical quotations expressing cruelty and racism are found to match Nazi ideas, but this match is considered incomplete.

1073. Zeckel, A. The totemistic significance of the unicorn. Wilbur, G. and Muensterberger, W. (eds.) *Psychoanalysis and Culture*. New York: International Universities Press, 1951.

The myth of the unicorn, well-known in European medieval art, is actually a universal story, found in many different versions all over the world. It is interpreted here as an Oedipal, totemistic fantasy. It is created through a distortion, by disguising the mother-son incest fantasy. The ambivalence felt towards the father is reflected in the desire to hunt the animal and then possess its unique horn, an obvious and impressive phallus.

1074.   Zeligs, D.F. Two episodes in the life of Jacob. *American Imago*, 1953, *10*, 181-203.

Despite the fact that she is well aware of Rank's truly psychoanalytic interpretations, Zeligs still prefers to treat the mythological Jacob as a "real person". The results are not especially enlightening.

1075.   Zeligs, D. Abraham and monotheism. *American Imago*, 1954, *11*, 193-316.

A myth is taken to be history cum biography, and Abraham's "personality" is discussed.

1076.   Zeligs, D.F. The personality of Joseph. *American Imago*, 1955, *12*, 47-69.

Once again, a myth is taken to be history cum biography, and Joseph's "personality" is discussed.

1077.   Zeligs, D.F. A character study of Samuel. *American Imago*, 1955, *12*, 355-386.

1078.   Zeligs, D.F. Saul, the tragic king. *American Imago*, 1957, *14*, 61-100.

Saul, a purely mythological figure, is described and discussed here as a real person and a real personality, with conscious and unconscious parts.

1079.   Zeligs, D.F. A study of King David. *American Imago*, 1960, *17*, 179-200.

1080.   Zeligs, D.F. The mother in Hebrew Monotheism. *The Psychoanalytic Study of Society*, 1960, *1*, 287-311.

Analyzes a variety of Biblical texts and Jewish legends, but leaves the reader confused between mythology and history.

1081.   Zeligs, D.F. Solomon: man and myth. *Psychoanalysis and the Psychoanalytic Review*, 1961, *48*, 77-103, 91-110.

1082.   Zeligs, D.F. The family romance of Moses: I The "personal myth". *American Imago*, 1966, *23*, 110-131.

1083.   Zeligs, D.F. Moses in Midian: the burning bush. *American Imago*, 1969, *26*, 379-400.

1084.   Zeligs, D.F. Moses and pharaoh: A psychoanalytic study of their encounter. *American Imago*, 1973, *30*, 192-220.

Here again, Moses is not only considered a historical figure, but we are invited to look at his "psyche" and personality dynamics.

1085.   Zeligs, D.F. *Psychoanalysis and the Bible*. New York: Bloch Publishing Co., 1974. (also New York: Human Sciences Press, 1988).

This collection of articles published earlier and summarized above (see 1074-1084) is an example of how not to do psychoanalytic interpretations. Zeligs treats mythological figures, such as Joseph, as real individuals with real personalities, and so can describe their lives, experiences, and unconscious feelings. The whole approach is apologetic, uncritical, and childish, appropriate for Sunday School teaching.

For additional materials on this topic, see also 221, 318, 507, 527, 529, 540, 547, 551, 555, 556, 568, 601, 605, 902, 1106, 1113, 1134, 1144, 1212, 1304, 1305, 1306, 1307, 1313, 1316, 1321, 1322, 1328, 1331, 1343, 1344, 1344, 1347, 1413, 1505, 1506, 1514, 1521, 1522, 1524, 1526, 1527, 1609, 1801, 1915, 2008, 2009, 2102, 2102.

And see Sections 11, 13, 15.

11

RITUALS

1101.   Beidelman, T.O. The ox and Nuer sacrifice: Some Freudian hypotheses about Nuer symbolism. *Man*, 1966, *1*, 453-467.

Oxen, a neutered animal, are chosen as a beast of sacrifice in Nuer culture. This is interpreted as reflecting a cultural ideal of male controlled sexuality, expressed through the ritual castration of bulls.

1102.   Beit-Hallahmi, B. Sacrifice, fire, and the victory of the sun: A search for the origins of Hanukkah. *The Psychoanalytic Review*, 1977, *63*, 497-509.

Traces the origins of this festival to its dual sources. One in the astronomical event of the winter solstice, which has given rise to numerous festivals around the world, expressing anxieties and joys about the sun. The other is anxieties conflicts about sacrifice in general and human sacrifice in particular, a persistent theme in Judaic tradition. The final form of the Hanukkah ritual signifies a sublimated sacrifice of pure fire.

1103.   Carroll, M.P. Praying the rosary: The anal-erotic origins of a popular Catholic devotion. *Journal for the Scientific Study of Religion*, 1987, *26*, 486-498 (also in M.P. Carroll, *Catholic Cults and Devotions*. McGill-Queens Press, 1989).

Carroll interprets the popular Catholic ritual of the Rosary as expressing in sublimated form the child's desire to play with feces and enabling believers to obtain unconscious gratification of that desire.

1104.   Desmonde, W.H. The bull fight as a religious ritual. *American Imago*, 1952, *9*, 163-195.

This speculative interpretation seeks to show that the bullfighting ritual is a reenactment of the "primal crime". It suggests that the bullfight is a survival of the totem-feast, and the bull is both god and man. At the same time, any animal sacrifice is viewed as representing the killing of both father and son; first the primal crime, and then its atonement.

1105. Desmonde, W.H. The Eleusian mysteries. *Journal of the Hillside Hospital*, 1952, *1*, 204-218.

The mysteries, famous and enigmatic, are interpreted as growing out of pre-historical puberty rites, which are always ritual aimed at overcoming Oedipal ambivalence.

1106. Desmonde, W.H. *Magic, Myth and Money: The Origin of Money in Religious Ritual*. New York: Free Press of Glencoe, 1962.

This essay on the connection between money and religious traditions contains many references to classical Greek mythology and religion, as well as to religion in traditional societies. Special attention is paid to totemism, as well as other Freudian ideas.

1107. DeVos, G. and Suarez-Orozco, M. Sacrifice and the experience of power. *Journal of Psychoanalytic Anthropology*, 1987, *10*, 309-340.

Sacrifice is not only a solution for a developmental problem (according to classical psychoanalytic formulations) or a continuation of the totemic pattern of atoning for the primal crime (as proposed in *Totem and Taboo*). It can also be a magical way of gaining power from supernatural forces. This may be temporary, but the feeling of power and confidence may be beneficial for the participants. In addition to this original formulation, the article contains an excellent literature survey.

1108. Dundes, A. Summoning deity through ritual fasting. *American Imago*, 1963, *20*, 213-220.

Ritual fasting as a means of achieving contact with the supernatural is found in several North American tribes. Following the logic of the culture and personality theory, which predicts differences in culture and personality according to child rearing practices, this custom is explained. It is to be found indeed in cultures where the baby experiences periods of hunger, followed by parental caring. Thus there is an association between deprivation and parental support. Later, the deified parent is expected to respond under similar circumstances. Fasting may also induce visions, which will only reinforce this connection. This is an excellent example of the effective use of cultural data.

1109. Dundes, A. A psychoanalytic study of the bullroarer. *Man*, 1976, *11*, 220-238.

The bullroarer, which may seem like a common toy, is actually an ancient and widely spread sacred symbol. Following insights suggested by Ernest Jones, the bullroarer and its use in male initiation rites are interpreted as being connected to ideas of pregnancy envy, anal eroticism, and ritual homosexuality. Though some etymological interpretations seem farfetched, there are many stimulating ideas which may be applied to other initiation practices around the world.

1110. Erikson, E.H. Ontogeny of ritualization. In R.M. Lowesenstein et al. (eds.) *Psychoanalysis -- A General Psychology: Essays in Honor of Heinz Hartmann*. New York: International Universities Press, 1966.

According to the hypothesis presented here, the ritualization of hope is based on the interaction between mother and baby during the first year of life. Periodical reassurances of hope are given by religious rituals.

1111. Erikson, E.H. *Toys and Reasons: Stages in the Ritualization of Experience.* New York: Norton, 1977.

Here ritual is defined as a tendency "... to use objects endowed with special and symbolic meanings for the representation of an imagined scene in a circumscribed sphere" (p. 42-43). This is connected with similar tendencies in animal behavior. The normal process of ritualization in everyday life is then linked to the psychodynamics of religion and its rituals (see 1110 above).

1112. Feldman, S. S. Notes on some religious rites and ceremonies. *Journal of the Hillside Hospital,* 1959, *8,* 36-41.

Following Freud's (1907) discussion of religious ritual in relation to individual neurosis, Feldman sets out to amplify and illustrate the original ideas. While religious ritual shares basic psychological mechanisms with neurosis (and may appear bizarre to non-believers), it does have historical and collective origins. While the religious person observes the ritual, and feels pleased, the neurotic follows his compulsions and feels tortured and doubtful. Clinical cases show that religious neurotics may endow certain traditional rituals with personal meaning. That is a result of their neurosis, not of the rituals!

1113. Fraiberg, L. and Fraiberg, S. Hallowe'en: Ritual and myth in a children's holiday. *American Imago,* 1950, *7,* 289-327.

This article contains a thorough survey of Hallowe'en customs in the United States, their classification and interpretation. Traditional activities on Hallowe'en night involve fires, supernatural beings, dead ancestors, witches, harvest customs. These activities are interpreted as reflecting the "great primal drama of killing and eating the father". For US children, Hallowe'en is a night of licensed aggression towards parental figures, expressing Oedipal wishes. This interpretation is a true classic, a model for looking at ritual acts.

1114. Garma, A. The origin of clothes. *The Psychoanalytic Quarterly,* 1949, *18,* 173-190.

The author moves from a general, and convincing, interpretation of clothes as unconscious substitutes for foetal membranes and symbolizing maternal protection to an attempt at interpreting Jewish ritual objects. Here he is much less successful. Example: he believes that the Hebrew word Zizit (for fringes) is related to the Yiddish or German words for breasts. It is this kind of sloppy research which gives psychoanalytic interpretation a bad name.

1115. Gay, V.P. Psychopathology and ritual: Freud's essay "Obsessive actions and religious practices". *Psychoanalytic Review,* 1975, *62,* 493-507.

This is a meticulous, scholarly, and devastating critique of Freud's 1907 paper. Relying on a close reading of the original German text, Gay concludes that religious practices are indeed different from obsessive actions. One reason is the consciousness of guilt, which may exist in the religious person, but is repressed in the obsessive. Another is the religious meaning of the ritual, which may be known to the believer, as transmitted by the culture.

1116.   Gay, V.P. *Freud on Ritual: Reconstruction and Critique*. Missoula, MT: Scholars Press, 1979.

Gay criticizes Freud for ignoring, after 1907 (e.g. in *Totem and Taboo*, 1913) an important distinction made in the original essay on religious ritual and compulsive neurosis. This was the contrast between religious ritual, which is the consequence of conscious suppression, or voluntary renunciation, and the neurotic "ritual", which is a consequence of unconscious, involuntary, repression.

1117.   Girard, R. *Violence and the Sacred*. Baltimore: Johns Hopkins University Press, 1977.

Offers a general theory of the origins of sacrifice and religion. The act of sacrifice, which involves killing an animal, is interpreted as a magical act aiming at a displacement of violence from society into the victim. Human aggressive impulses are projected onto sacred beings and their injunctions. The scapegoat plays a major role in the process, as all sins are projected on it.

1118.   Graber, R.B. and Forsyth, D.W. Psychoanalytic speculations on horse-and-buggy sectarianism. *Journal of Psychoanalytic Anthropology*, 1986, *9*, 121-142.

This article offers speculations about the traditions of groups such as the conservative Mennonites, Amish, and Brethren in the United States. Prohibitions against the use of automobiles and electricity, and traditional consumption habits are interpreted as defenses against sexual urges, specifically Oedipal.

1119.   Greenberg, D. and Witztum, E. The treatment of obsessive-compulsive disorder in strictly religious patients. In M.T. Pato and J. Zohar (eds.) *Current Treatments of Obsessive-Compulsive Disorder*. Washington, DC: American Psychiatric Press, 1991.

This is the most comprehensive survey of the clinical phenomenon of compulsive behavior in religious individuals, with many references to the Freudian hypothesis about the connection between compulsion and religious rituals.

1120.   Heimbrock, H.G. Ritual and transformation: A psychoanalytic interpretation. In H.G. Heimbrock and H.B. Boudewijnse (eds.) *Current Studies on Rituals: Perspectives for the Psychology of Religion*. Amsterdam: Rodopi, 1990.

Attempts to apply Winnicott's often-cited concept of transitional states and transitional objects to religious ritual, as "... through ritual means individuals and groups try to elaborate an experiential space between the self and reality analogous to the early transitional sphere . Added to other attempts to apply Winnicott's ideas, this is an original, stimulating, contribution.'

1121. Jones, E. The symbolic significance of salt in folklore and superstition (1912). In E. Jones, *Essays in Applied Psychoanalysis*. London: The Hogarth Press and the Institute of Psychoanalysis, 1951, vol. 2.

This is a far-ranging survey of the magical uses of salt, considered to be a symbol of both semen and urine, and its place in culture, all over the world. In various religious traditions it has been used for sacrificial offerings. Holy water in the Roman Catholic Church contains salt, and it is used for ritual purification through symbolic rebirth. This liquid is interpreted as symbolizing both paternal semen and uterine waters. Baptism also imbues the subject with the magical properties of the holy water. It is also suggested that urine was originally used in all such ceremonies. [Cow's urine is still used in purification ceremonies among the Parsees in India, and its drinking is recommended as a cure-all by some Hindus]. These practices, and the symbolic ideas behind them, stem from infantile notions of sexual intercourse and pregnancy. Here is the connection between early childhood fantasies, adult unconscious associations, culture, and ritual is ingeniously illustrated.

1122. Jones, I.H. Subincision among Australian western desert aborigines. *British Journal of Medical Psychology*, 1969, *42*, 183-190.

This critical article rejects psychoanalytic explanations of male genital mutilation in favor of a cultural one: these operations serve as means of powerful group identification, after having been initiated for unclear reasons.

1123. Kiev, A. Ritual goat sacrifice in Haiti. *American Imago*, 1962, *19*, 349-359.

This is a fascinating and insightful case study, worthy not only because of its classical psychoanalytic approach but also because of the incisive social analysis. We get here first a real picture of life in Haiti, and the material conditions which give rise to the power of Voodoo. The ritual sacrifice described here is viewed as a totem feast. On one level a symbolic murder of a divinely possessed animal. It maintains both social control, exercised by the Voodoo priest, by allowing the followers some emotional relief. The sacrifice is both a relief and a threat, as the priest reminds his followers of his "supernatural" ability to kill them.

1124. Kurylyk, E. *Veronica and Her Cloth: History, Symbolism, and Structure of a "True" Image*. Cambridge, MA: Basil Blackwell, 1991.

While structuralist in orientation, this study uses psychoanalytic interpretations to deal with the symbolism and the meaning of menstruation in Western religious traditions.

1125. La Barre, W. *They Shall Take Up Serpents*. Minneapolis: University of Minnesota Press, 1962.

This is an attempt to apply psychoanalytic interpretation to a fascinating form of Christian ritual native to the United States: snake handling. This practice has been observed since the early twentieth century among poor whites in Appalachia. La Barre, while admitting overdetermination in snake symbolism (father, death, aggression) emphasizes snakes as phallic symbols and snake handling as sexual excitement.

1126. Lorand, S. The anathema of the dead mother. In G. Roheim (ed.) *Psychoanalysis and the Social Sciences*. New York: International Universities Press, 1947.

An unusual ceremony in which a woman who dies during pregnancy is required to give up the unborn child through a mock trial is the starting point for a discussion of anxieties and taboos surrounding death. Because the death of a loved one is the source of ambivalence and projected hostility, various rituals serve to keep those under control, while allowing partial expression of fear and hostility. Protecting the community from evil spirits and from its own members' evil impulses is one of religion's most important roles.

1127. Merkur, D. The psychodynamics of the Navajo Coyoteway ceremonial. *Journal of Mind and Behavior*, 1981, 2, 243-257.

Navajo "instrumental" ritualism, used to prepare hunters for their job, is analyzed here in terms of associated anxieties and conflicts. The rituals are shown to be effective in relieving stress and anxiety. This case study should have important implications for other cultural contexts.

1128. Money-Kryle, R. *The Meaning of Sacrifice*. London: The Hogarth Press and the Institute of Psychoanalysis, 1930.

Following *Totem and Taboo*, Money-Kryle analyzes sacrifice as a neurotic symptom. It is interpreted as a repetition (and commemoration) of the cannibalistic killing of the father in totemic rituals, through which ambivalent feelings toward the father are expressed. Sacrifice takes place not because of the "Primal Sin", but because of ontogenetic factors. Many unconscious fantasies are satisfied by the killing of an animal: killing the father, the self, the mother, etc. Killing expresses hate, while eating expresses love and identification.

1129. Palm, R. On the symbolic significance of the Star of David. *American Imago*, 1958, *15*, 227-231.

The Star of David, an ancient talisman composed of two triangles, and in recent centuries adopted as a symbol of Jews or Judaism, is interpreted as an emblem of bisexuality. The idea of omnipotence, ascribed to the gods, is expressed by two sets of genitals, male and female, which defend against castration. This hypothesis leaves the adoption of this talisman by Jews unexplained.

1130. Paul, R.A. The Sherpa temple as a model of the psyche. *American Ethnologist*, 1976, *3*, 131-146.

This is a detailed piece of anthropological observation, focusing on a temple building and its appointments. A Sherpa Buddhist temple in Northeastern Nepal, a well-defined and unique sacred space, is interpreted as an objectification of a Sherpa model of the mind, and of the subjective internal experience of the Sherpa in religious activity. This tri-partite model, separating lower desires from upper controls, can be compared with the psychoanalytic structural model.

1131. Paul, R.A. A mantra and its meaning. *The Psychoanalytic Study of Society*, 1981, 9, 85-91.

The famous mantra Om Mani Padmi Om, known throughout India and Tibet, and originating in Sanskrit, is interpreted here as expressing the desire and contentment of the baby at his mother's breast. It is tied to the primordial sounds of ma and pa, also stemming from breast feeding. The bliss of oral gratification is eroticized through repetition of the mantra, which is also compared with the Catholic rosary formula, a more explicit rendering of the mother-child relationship.

1132. Pearson, G.H.J. A note on the medusa: A speculative attempt to explain a ritual. *Bulletin of the Philadelphia Association for Psychoanalysis*, 1967, *17*, 1-9.

The ritual display of female genitals, reported in ancient legends and myths, in contemporary traditional cultures, (and also in clinical non-ritual cases), is interpreted as a castration warning. Its motive is the magical attempt to ward off evil spirits. This speculative interpretation seems to be quite convincing in its understanding of magical thinking.

1133. Pollock, R.E. Some psychoanalytic considerations of bull fighting and bull worship. *Israel Annals of Psychiatry and Related Disciplines*, 1974, *12*, 53-67.

Bull-gods and bull worship are found in most Mediterranean cultures as well as in South Asia. The ritualized killing of a bull is an ancient tradition which survives to this day in a secular form in Latin America and in Latin Europe. The interpretation offered here emphasizes overdetermination. Bulls were deified, but also killed, and worshipped while being consumed. The same ambivalence, emotional and practical, is expressed in ritualized killing. This is a ritual fight with paternal authority and might. It may represent also sibling rivalry and sexuality. The matador in the modern corrida is somewhat feminine in dress and gestures, but also phallic in his actions. The corrida is both a primal scene enactment and a life-death drama, thus giving the audience as much excitement as any work of art of ecstatic religious rituals.

1134. Redl, F. Fritz Redl on "Den Heiligen Nikolaus", In A.D. de Groot, *Saint Nicholas: A Psychoanalytic Study of His History and Myth*. Hague: Mouton, 1965.

While accepting the idea that sexual and aggressive derives have something to do with the elaborate ritual cum myth of Santa, Redl suggests that it has much to do with the interpersonal constellation between the world of children and the world of adults. Thus, it is a ritual which acts out mythic themes of power, sin, and justice. This is an important notion, pointing out that children are less than innocent in more than just one way.

1135. Roheim, G. The covenant of Abraham. *The International Journal of Psychoanalysis*, 1939, *20*, 452-459.

The ancient ritual of covenanting through the cutting of a victim through the middle, mentioned in the Hebrew Bible but known elsewhere, is interpreted in a thoroughly new way, with the help of clinical material. After presenting numerous example of this magical ritual, Roheim seems to anticipate the theoretical ideas of Melanie Klein and Margaret Mahler in offering an early object relations explanation. The fantasy of opening up the mother's body, appearing in analysand's free associations, is tied to a fantasy of finding "good body contents" inside. The ritual, sublimating these early fantasies, reinforces feelings of security and fantasies of reparation, as destruction is followed by the promise of future life.

1136.   Saffady, W. Fears of sexual license during the English Reformation. *History of Childhood Quarterly*, 1973, *1*, 89-96.

Following Freud's discussion of the connection between religious rituals, obsessive rituals, and impulse control, the author sets out to analyze Protestant conservatism in Reformation England. The article suggests that resistance to more radical Protestantism stemmed from fears that giving up traditional rituals would be followed by unrestrained aggression and sexuality.

1137.   Schlesinger, K. Origins of the Passover Seder in ritual sacrifice. *The Psychoanalytic Study of Society*, 1976, *7*, 369-399.

Ritual is conceptualized as emerging from a combination of the individual's need for release of aggressive and libidinal drives and the community's need for binding rituals, contributing to group cohesion and adaptation. Ritual patterns are creative breakthroughs (coming from the unconscious) which will survive or perish in accordance with their adaptive value to the group.

The Passover ritual meal, as celebrated by Jews since the Middle Ages, is interpreted as containing many archaic elements, including references to child sacrifice. Much historical and linguistic material is presented here, and some of it is clearly misinterpreted.

1138.   Schneiderman, L. A theory of repression in the light of archaic religion. *Psychoanalytic Review*, 1966, *53*, 220-232.

The conflict between fertility rites and sexuality is described in relation to traditions of mother goddesses and their worship. Fertility rituals are tied to an opposition to free sexuality, because fertility rites, often tied to mourning, demand the sacrifice of human individuality and pleasure.

1139.   Seda Bonilla, E. Spiritualism, psychoanalysis and psychodrama. *American Anthropologist*, 1969, *71*, 493-497.

One spiritualist session, witnessed by the author in 1958 is analyzed within the framework of psychodrama and psychoanalysis. The session enacts intrapsychic conflicts dramatically. On an allegorical level, the process represents the patient's repressed feelings, which are verbalized by the spiritualist, a benevolent parental surrogate. The therapeutic ritual achieves its aims by supporting the patient's ego and offering an acceptable conception of internal suffering, externalized as spirit-possession.

1140.   Siegel, L.M. A bar to conversion. *The Psychoanalytic Review*, 1966, *53*, 16-23.

The strong Judaic taboos regarding blood are interpreted as a psychological measure to prevent the re-enactment of the primal crime (*Totem and Taboo*). Blood itself became an extension of the primordial deity. The Christian Eucharist, which involved the symbolic drinking of blood, is one major reason why Christianity has been rejected by Jews over the past two millennia. This is interpreted as an "unconscious dread of symbolic deicide", experienced by Jews.

1141.   Sterba, R. On Christmas. *The Psychoanalytic Quarterly*, 1944, *13*, 79-83.

The Christmas festival, focused on the birth of Jesus Christ, is interpreted here as an acting-out of infantile fantasies about childbirth, as shown by the "pregnant" Santa, who arrives through the chimney to deliver gifts prepared in secrecy. Emotional reactions to Christmas have to do with this unconscious meaning.

1142.   Tarachow, S. Totem feast in modern dress. *American Imago*, 1948, *5*, 65-69.

Secular banquets, a ritual common in the life of modern professionals and academics, are analyzed as a variant of the totem meal. The eating has little of its original flavor, but the struggle with authority is there, directed towards the honored speaker, who is also the target of hostility.

1143.   Troisiers, J. Menirs, trilithons and dolmens: Their symbolism. *British Journal of Medical Psychology*, 1932, *12*, 337-342.

Offers an interpretation of pre-historic monolithic monuments. Tied to early totemic rituals, they represent male and female genitals, or mother and father. Modern monuments, such as the Arc de Triomphe, still represent the mother, while similar masculine monuments are found everywhere.

1144.   Walsh, M.N. A psychoanalytic interpretation of a primitive dramatic ritual. *Journal of the Hillside Hospital*, 1962, *11*, 3-20.

This is an interpretation of a Hopi ritual which acts out a traditional myth. It is viewed here as an institutionalized opportunity for acting out individual intrapsychic conflicts.

The numerous deities in the Hopi pantheon are interpreted as representing various aspects of the main figures in the Oedipal situation. The plumed serpent represents the erect parental penis, but is also the fructifying and fertilizing principle of nature. Children, represented by the sprouted corn, are threatened by the father's power. There is also a pre-genital regression with a representation of the phallic mother. The interpretation is supported by material from individual psychoanalysis.

1145.   Wayne, R. A little religious ceremonial. *American Imago*, 1954, *11*, 194-202.

The ritual in question, observed in Italy, consists of touching a saint's tomb with a rigidly outstretched left arm, while covering one's eyes with the right hand. It is interpreted as a wish for the father's penis, or the father's phallic power, simultaneously denied by a symbolic castration. Undoubtedly, overdetermination is called for in this case.

For additional materials on this topic, see also 318, 332, 333, 502, 503, 510, 513, 521, 527, 540, 548, 551, 555, 557, 564, 569, 605, 610, 632, 1029, 1035, 1048, 1057, 1065, 1067, 1301, 1302, 1304, 1311, 1315, 1322, 1339, 1340, 1341, 1343, 1349, 1501, 1503, 1504, 1513, 1515, 1523, 1526, 1609, 1610, 1812, 1906, 2003, 2008, 2009.

And see sections 10, 12.

12

TRANSITION RITES

1201.   Arlow, J.A. A psychoanalytic study of a religious initiation rite. *The Psychoanalytic Study of the Child*, 1951, *6*, 353-374.

Using clinical data taken from contemporary U.S. Jewish clients, as well as historical information, the author looks at a traditional initiation ritual which has survived in the midst of modern society. It is found that it gives rise to sibling rivalry, penis envy, and other family tensions. The implied transition to sexual maturity is a major source of anxiety. When casting off paternal authority is too frightening, it is possible that a religious conversion will follow.

1202.   Daly, C.D. The psycho-biological origins of circumcision. *International Journal of Psychoanalysis*, 1950, *31*, 217-236.

Suggests that the function of circumcision in males and of clitoridectomy in females is to eradicate the bisexuality which results from the traumatic frustration of heterosexual impulses in the Oedipal repression of incest. These mutilations represent a second wave of repression which leads boys to re-identify with men, and girls to re-identify with women.

1203.   Maler, M. The Jewish Orthodox circumcision ceremony: Its meaning from direct study of the rite. *Journal of the American Psychoanalytic Association*, 1966, *14*, 510-517.

The circumcision ceremony is a generational affair. It involves the father no less than the son, and invokes in the father his own Oedipal strivings and anxieties. In Jewish tradition, the father is expected to perform the operation himself. An important part of the ceremony is the sucking of blood from the penis, a homosexual act. It is concluded that the circumcision ceremony is a condensed defensive maneuver on the part of the father against his own castration anxieties, aroused by the birth of an Oedipal rival.

1204.   Nunberg, H. Circumcision and problems of bisexuality. *International Journal of Psycho-Analysis*, 1947, *28*, 145-179.

To arrive at the unconscious meaning of circumcision, Nunberg uses materials taken from numerous clinical cases, including dreams. The conclusions are that it is tied to conflicts around sexual identity and the genitals, as well as pre-genital experiences and impulses. Traditions of circumcisions represent a solution to a homosexual attachment to the father, rebellion, and submission. In the case of Judaism, the custom expresses submission to the father. Sacrificing a part of the penis demonstrates love to both father and God.

1205.   Nunberg, H. *Problems of Bisexuality as Reflected in Circumcision.* London: Imago Publishing, 1949.

From clinical material, it is concluded that being circumcised was tied to bisexual fantasies, and there are also fantasies of the foreskin as representing femininity. Historical material is interpreted in the light of clinical data. Christian opposition to the Jewish custom of circumcision is interpreted as evolving from a homosexual tie to the father. Abandoning circumcision means weakening the homosexual tie to the father, opening the door to the pagan worship of mother and son figures. This is indeed what happened in the history of early Christianity. In addition to the interpretations of the ritual, Nunberg tends to speculate about the individual psychodynamics of Paul, which seems unjustified.

1206.   Nunberg, H. Problems of bisexuality as reflected in circumcision. in H. Nunberg, *Practice and Theory of Psychoanalysis.* Vol. II. New York: International Universities Press, 1965.

Suggests that while the foreskin is a symbolic residue of femininity, its removal is also a symbolic substitute for castration.

1207.   Reik, T. Puberty rites among savages: On some similarities in the mental life of savages and neurotics. In T. Reik, *Ritual, Psychoanalytic Studies.* New York: International Universities Press, 1958.

Circumcision and death rites attempt a resolution of the conflict between fathers and sons. Incest and patricide are dealt with through puberty rites. Two themes are prominent in puberty rites: the killing and rebirth of the initiate, and the infliction of circumcision or other genital mutilation. The "killing", and the mutilations, are interpreted as atonement for the primal crime (*Totem and Taboo*) and threats designed to prevent incest and parricide. The rebirth is a birth from the father, expressing a complete masculine identification. Nullifying the birth from a woman is supposed to eliminate incestuous desires as well. The "resurrection" of the sons represents the undoing the fathers' wishes to kill their own fathers.

1208.   Reik, T. Psychoanalytic studies of Bible Exegesis I. The wrestling of Jacob. In T. Reik, *Dogma and Compulsion: Psychoanalytic Studies of Religion and Myths.* New York: International Universities Press, 1951.

Reik interprets both Jacob's dream and Jacob's wrestling with the angel as mythical expressions and reflections of ancient initiation rites. The rites themselves were a dramatic enactment of the male's conflict over the renunciation of incestous wishes and the movement towards independence. This is done by an initial attack and mutilation, followed by acceptance and blessing.

1209. Roheim, G. Dying gods and puberty ceremonies. *Journal of the Royal Anthropological Institute*, 1929, *59*, 181-197.

This study utilizes anthropological data from contemporary traditional societies, as well as historical findings. Ancient traditions of the young, dying god in West Asia are surveyed, and interpreted as stemming from pre-historical initiation rites.

1210. Roheim, G. Transition rites. *Psychoanalytic Quarterly*, 1942, *11*, 336-374.

Transition rites in traditional societies, especially those focusing on birth and puberty, are surveyed as reflecting separation anxiety. This anxiety, considered the primal form of all human anxieties, is dealt with and transformed through the rites, which create new object relations.

1211. Schlossman, H.H. Circumcision as defense: A study in psychoanalysis and religion. *The Psychoanalytic Quarterly*, 1966, *35*, 340-356.

Using a clinical case study, together with historical and mythological material (as the author consistently confuses religious mythology and history), it is suggested that circumcision is a form of sacrifice. It represents a defense against castration through a token sacrifice. It is part of a masochistic submission pattern, as well as a mark of relative progress from human sacrifice, through self castration, to minimal mutilation.

1212. Schneiderman, L. The cult of Osiris in relation to primitive initiation rites. *The Psychoanalytic Review*, 1965, *52*, 38-50.

Following Reik's theory of ritual, the ancient Egyptian cult surrounding the myth of Osiris is interpreted as having grown out of tribal initiation rites, and the figure of Osiris himself to represent a preoccupation with death, but also an affirmation of life.

1213. Yazmajian, R.V. A circumcision fantasy. *Psychoanalytic Quarterly*, 1965, *39*, 108-110.

Reports a rare fantasy found among Jews in analytical treatment. It consists of the denial of the physical meaning of circumcision. Some individuals imagine that it involves only a dorsal incision in the prepuce, and not its complete removal. Thus, mutilation is considered minimal, and the penis is imagined to be better protected. In 2 clinical cases this denial fantasy was accompanied by exhibitionist behavior. The implications in terms of castration anxiety seem to be clear.

1214. Zegans, S. and Zegans, L.S. Bar Mitzvah: A rite for a transitional age. *Psychoanalytic Review*, 1973, *66*, 115-132.

This article interprets the rite in terms of ego psychology and identity theory, and suggests that the ceremony and preparations for it enable the boy to express doubts about competence and mastery, then to be overcome.

1215. Zimmermann, F. Origin and significance of the Jewish rite of circumcision. *Psychoanalytic Review*, 1951, *38*, 103-112.

Offers two possible explanations for the specific Jewish pattern of circumcision: its performance on infants and the custom of sucking the blood. Sucking another man's blood was part of a covenant ceremony, here serving to overcome the father's hostility, expressed more directly in the mutilation itself. Another origin is in the wish to encourage sexuality and fertility, through the creation of a "permanent erection".

For additional materials on this topic, see also 502, 551, 1011, 1011, 1052, 1055, 1105, 1122, 1126, 1324, 1329, 1336, 1340, 1348, 1407, 1421, 1609, 2003, 2006.

13

JUDAISM

1301. Abraham K. The Day of Atonement: Some observations on Reik's *Problems of the Psychology of Religion*. In K. Abraham *Clinical Papers and Essays On Psycho-Analysis*. London: Hogarth Press, 1955. (Original German version 1920).

Abraham supports Reik's interpretation of the Jewish Day of Atonement and offers additional evidence for this explanation. "The Kol Nidre is the substitute for the extreme violence directed against the father-god, for the totem meal, which is followed by the great act of atonement...." Moreover, Abraham points to the custom of sacrificing a cock (for men) or a hen (for women) as an expiatory offering, which is another repetition of the totem meal, this time within the family circle.

1302. Almansi, R.J. A psychoanalytic interpretation of the Menorah. *Journal of the Hillside Hospital*, 1953, *2*, 80-95.

The seven-branched candelabra is interpreted as a derivation of the hollow sacrificial idol, each branch representing one of its seven facial orifices. The hollow idol was used in the sacrifice of the first-born. The candelabra with its base would represent the human body, particularly the father. Later the cruel idol was transformed into a light giving object, which could represent both male and female.

1303. Almansi, J. Ego-psychological implications of a religious symbol: A cultural and experimental study. *The Psychoanalytic Study of Society*, 1964, *3*, 39-70.

This article combines two studies. One is a traditional "psychoanalytic archeology" project, in which much historical and cultural evidence is produced to prove the hypothesis that the Tablets of the Law, mentioned in the Hebrew Bible, symbolized two human hands. Some of the archeological evidence is quite striking, and the author may be onto something, but we are lost in a mire of speculation, and the author too often accepts Biblical mythology as history. The second part is a tachistoscopic study of the same symbol, done on 10 psychiatric inpatients. The idea is intriguing, and may be worth repeating, but the reader is left with many questions about this particular application of it (e.g. why were schizophrenic inpatients selected?).

1304.   Almansi, R.J. A further contribution to the psychoanalytic interpretation of the Menorah. *Journal of the Hillside Hospital*, 1954, *3*, 3-18.

Following an earlier article (see 1302 above), which interpreted the seven-branched candelabra, this article explores the unconscious meanings of the number seven, the Second Commandment, and the Biblical Golden Calf story. It is speculated that originally the number seven represented absolute evil. The Sabbath was originally an unlucky, tabooed day. Ancient customs of Human sacrifice and fear of the gods are the source of later changes in meaning of these images.

1305.   Beit-Hallahmi, B. The foundations of Judaism: Psychoanalytic interpretations. *Israel Journal of Psychiatry*, 1993,

This is a critical survey of 40 psychoanalytic contributions to the issue of the sources and beginnings of historical Judaism. Ideas regarding early totemism, mother-worship, and Oedipal projections are reviewed.

1306.   Brenner, A.B. The covenant with Abraham. *The Psychoanalytic Review*, 1952, *39*, 34-52.

It has been observed that ancient Judaism has attempted to repress any memory of Oedipal strivings and totemic rites. This would lead to a conflicted, repressed culture, but Judaism seemed to have survived and adapted quite well. How is this to be explained? The speculative answer offered here deals with two main processes. First, the Covenant was an Oedipal permission to reach genitality, possibly at the small price of ritual circumcision. Then, Hebraism arrived at a more mature identification with the Father-God by the introjection and internalization, not of his symbolic flesh, but of his authority and moral standards. This made possible the development of a mature superego, without primal horde anxiety.

1307.   Brenner, A.B. Onan, the levirate marriage and the genealogy of the Messiah. *Journal of the American Psychoanalytic Association*, 1962, *10*, 701-721.

Compared to other mythologies, the Hebrew Bible makes an effort to suppress Oedipal subject matter, but the theme resurfaces time and again. The institution of levirate marriage (marriage of a man's childless widow to his brother), which is part of the Judaic tradition, but can be found elsewhere, is interpreted as reflecting repressed incest wishes. The myth of Tamar and the three brothers, found in chapter 28 of Genesis, is shown to include many vestiges of ancient cults and traditions, which reveal Oedipal preoccupations. It is noteworthy that Tamar's incestuous union has been selected to start the genealogy of David, the legendary king, and then of Jesus in Christian mythology.

1308.   Brink, L. Critical review: Frazer's Folk-lore in the Old Testament. *Psychoanalytic Review*, 1922, *9*, 218-254.

The universal mythological themes collected by Frazer are analyzed as reflecting infantile pre-genital and genital preoccupations within a dreamwork mechanism. This early article may seem to us hopelessly naive, reflecting an "evolutionary" view of humankind (borrowed from Freud) and mixing mythology and history. Still, it does contain some useful insights and underlines the reality of overdetermination in cultural productions.

1309.   Chandler, T. Ikhnaton and Moses. *American Imago*, 1962, *19*, 127-139.

Speculates that the Egyptian king Ikhnaton influenced "Moses" in the creation of Judaic monotheism, and points to many parallels between Ikhnaton's ideas and Biblical literature. The article's whole frame of reference is identical to that of *Moses and Monotheism*.

1310.   Cohen, S. The ontogenesis of prophetic behavior: A study in creative conscience formation. *Psychoanalysis and Psychoanalytic Review*, 1962, *40*, 100-122.

From the texts attributed to ancient prophets in the Hebrew Bible, the author has attempted to investigate the "thought processes" and the "formation of an autonomous creative conscience" in the individuals supposedly involved. This effort is inspired by existential psychotherapy and ignores completely the fictional nature of the ancient texts and the literary and religious conventions which shaped them.

1311.   Eder, M.D. The Jewish phylacteries and other Jewish ritual observances. *International Journal of Psychoanalysis*, 1933, *14*, 341-375.

Clinical material focusing on the Jewish phylacteries and related objects, produced by analysands who were of Jewish Orthodox background, but mostly non-observant, is presented in an attempt to ascertain the totemic origins of these artifacts. It is found that these objects are taken to be father-symbols, and are associated with friction between father and son. This is interpreted as showing a psychological complex tied to ancient totemic rituals, related to the primal father. Reik's view of the totemic ceremony, in which the faithful dressed themselves to look like the totem-god, is considered vindicated by the clinical findings. An alternative explanation would be that these artifacts come to symbolize father because children observe their fathers putting them on, which is a clear male prerogative. At age 13, when boys are enjoined to start using them, this is clearly an initiation into manhood.

1312.   Feldman, A. A. Freud's *Moses and Monotheism* and the three states of Israelitish religion. *The Psychoanalytic Review*, 1944, *31*, 361-418.

This is an original, provocative and impressive work, published posthumously. The author died in 1941, and so we can assume that his extensive research was done in the 1930s. We are presented here with an ambitious attempt to reconstruct the history of Judaism, which elegantly demolishes Freud's thesis in *Moses and Monotheism*. Feldman's main difference with Freud is that he approaches the Hebrew Bible as a collection of mythological sources, to be interpreted in a historical context. Accordingly, he does not believe in the historicity of either

Moses or the Exodus from Egypt. The history of Judaism is divided by Feldman into 3 periods:
1. Canaanite "Mother and Child" religion.
2. Torah Judaism, initiated by Ezra around 450 BCE.
3. Rabbinical Judaism, started around 200 BCE.
While Ezra attempted to suppress the original "Mother and Child" religion, without success, it was rabbinical Judaism that kept many matriarchal and dying-god traditions. The survival of Judaism and the amazing vitality of Jewish traditions are explained not as the result of obedience to the one and only Father God, but just the opposite. It is the archaic, "pagan" elements in Judaism that have kept it alive. Judaism as we know, according to Feldman, is very much a sanctuary of "Mother and Child" rituals, which allow expression of irrepressible "primitive" impulses. Feldman's thesis about the history of Judaism seems more plausible than Freud's. His knowledge of living Judaism is clearly much more intimate than Freud's, despite many interpretations which will be disputed by scholars.

1313.   Feldman, A.A. The Davidic dynasty and the Davidic Messiah. *American Imago*, 1960, *17*, 163-178.

This posthumously published article deals with 2 separate topics, one historical and the other psychological. Regarding history, the author reaches the conclusion that Old Testament narratives (as well as Christianity) can be understood only against the background of the ancient cult of the Mother Goddess and her son-consort. Judaism attempted to suppress the mother-son part of this cult, but its elements and influences always resurfaced, as in the belief in David (actually dod), the once and future king of Judea, who will father the Messiah.

Regarding the psychological origins of the cult of the mother-goddess and her son-consort, and also of the father-god, it is suggested that these stem from childhood experiences and the triangle father-mother-child.

1314.   Feldman, A.B. The word in the beginning. *The Psychoanalytic Review*, 1964, *51*, 79-89.

An involved, convoluted, argument about the relationship between the name of the Judaic god YHVH and the first sound ever uttered by humans, by way of many bizarre hypotheses. This kind of logic puts to shame Athenian Sophists and medieval scholasticism. It has little to do with helping us to understand religion.

1315.   Feldman, S.S. The blessing of the Kohenites. *American Imago*, 1941, *2*, 296-322.

This detailed and complicated presentation attempts to offer an interpretation of an ancient Judaic ceremony, in which members of the priestly caste offer a sacred blessing to the people. It is suggested that the deep meaning of the ritual has to do with an assertion of parental authority, and a symbolic resolution of the Oedipal conflict.

1316.   Feldman, S.S. The sin of Reuben, first born son of Jacob. *Psychoanalysis and the Social Sciences*, 1955, *4*, 282-287.

Speculates about the Biblical legend of Reuben, who had intercourse with one of his father's concubines. The obvious Oedipal nature of the story is used to develop many groundless speculations.

1317.   Fodor, A. The origin of the Mosaic prohibition against cooking the suckling in its mother's milk. *International Journal of Psychoanalysis*, 1946, *27*, 140-144.

This is a critical response to Woolf (see 1349 below), which dealt with the same question. Fodor assumes that there was a matriarchal-matrilinear age, which preceded the coming of patriarchy. Both the prohibition on cooking a kid in its mother's milk, and the Judaic Passover ritual are expressions of the attempt to erase from memory and from practice the worship of female deities. This is a speculative article, with reasonable psychological premises, but with debatable historical evidence to support it. The notion of a matriarchal age seems totally untenable.

1318.   Fodor, A. Asherah of Ugarit. *American Imago*, 1952, *9*, 118-146.

Looking at archeological evidence, the author suggests that Canaanite religion had a syncretistic influence on ancient Judaism, and in this syncretism he seeks insight about the cult and the unconscious meaning of ancient mother goddesses. Traces of the cult of the Mother Goddess are found in Judaic rituals, especially in the Passover "alarm-ritual". Psychologically, we are reminded of the ambivalence towards earthly mothers which was projected into the Mother Goddesses, who represented both life and death.

1319.   Fodor, N. A personal analytic approach to the problem of the Holy Name. *The Psychoanalytic Review*, 1944, *31*, 165-180.

The interpretation is based on a unique form of self-analysis. Fodor kept a dream journal and recorded meticulously all his associations and interpretations of the dream elements.

In this way the meaning of the Judaic tetragrammaton is explored, and it is concluded that the holy name expresses the idea of the life force itself, thus confirming earlier interpretations achieved with much less effort.

1320.   Freehof, S.W. Three psychiatric stories from Rabbinic lore. *The Psychoanalytic Review*, 1942, *20*, 185-187.

These touching stories illustrate the sensitivity of some insightful rabbis. They seem to have shared something like Freud's earliest concept of psychotherapy: uncovering the original trauma leads to the disappearance of symptoms and guilt feelings.

1321.   Graves, R. and Patai, R. Some Hebrew myths and legends. *Encounter*, 1963, *20*, 3-18.

Offers insights into traditional Judaic myths by citing ancient Hebrew exegetes. In these early sources one can point to many quasi-psychoanalytic ideas. Ancient sages were suggesting bisexuality, incest, and similar motives as explanations for elements in myths.

1322. Grinberg, L. Psychoanalytic considerations on the Jewish Passover: Totemic sacrifice and meal. *American Imago*, 1962, *19*, 391-424.

Aims at showing that the Passover ritual originated in a totemic sacrifice, just like the Christian Eucharist. Such sacrifices, in which the god is ceremonially ingested, in the form of an animal, or of prepared food or bread, have been found in many cultures. It is interpreted here as tied to the infant's fantasy of devouring the mother's breast and body, according to Melanie Klein. Sacrificial rites in various forms express conflicts between aggression and guilt towards love objects. The article contains much historical information, as well as many speculative suggestions.

1323. Grollman, E.A. Some sights and insights of history, psychology and psychoanalysis concerning the Father-God and Mother-Goddess concepts in Judaism and Christianity. *American Imago*, 1963, *20*, 187-209.

This pedestrian effort surveys many bits of evidence regarding Mother-Goddess worship in ancient West Asia. It suggests that in pre-exilic Judaism the Mother-Goddess played a major role, and the formulation of Judaism as a Father-religion appeared only in the middle of the fifth century BCE. Judaism was a struggle against Mother worship, while Christianity was a regression to the dual unity of mother and son. It was also a regression to the idea of the resurrection of the dying god.

1324. Jones, E. The psychology of the Jewish question (1940). In E. Jones, *Essays in Applied Psychoanalysis*. London: The Hogarth Press and the Institute of Psychoanalysis, 1951.

Speculative discussion of Jewish history and the origins of anti-Semitism. Beyond historical speculations, Jones offers the hypothesis that ritual circumcision arouses castration fears. Jews are then perceived as individuals whose manliness has been impaired, and who, as a result, will use "effeminate", dishonest, ways to get what they want.

1325. Joseph. E.D. Cremation, fire, and oral aggression. *Psychoanalytic Quarterly*, 1960, *29*, 98-104.

The prohibition of cremation in Jewish tradition is interpreted in the light of both conscious and unconscious reasons. Consciously, Judaism believes in the physical resurrection of the body. Unconsciously, the taboo is tied to ancient cannibalistic rituals and to oral aggression.

1326. Katz, J. The Joseph dream anew. *Psychoanalytic Review*, 1963, *50*, 252-278.

Treats Joseph as a real-person, with conscious and unconscious experiences, blaming himself for his mother's death in childbirth, etc. Katz may have some interesting ideas about the meaning of Joseph's dreams, but it is unclear whether these reflect an anonymous author's unconscious, our unconscious, or Joseph's.

1327. Lorand, S. Dream interpretation in the Talmud. *International Journal of Psychoanalysis*, 1957, *38*, 92-97.

References to dream interpretation in the Talmud show that dreams were regarded as either prophetic or wish-fulfilling. The apparent similarity to some Freudian ideas is noted.

1328. Lourie, A. The Jewish god and the Greek hero. *American Imago*, 1948, *5*, 152-166.

A speculative attempt to arrive at the "Jewish personality" by way of comparing Judaic mythology with other traditions. Judaism adopts a certain solution of the Oedipus complex, while other national types follow other patterns of repression. Differences between Greek mythology and Biblical mythology are presented (father denial in the former, mother denial in the latter), and the conclusion is that in Jewish tradition "filial submission" is strongest, compared to other cultures.

1329. Lustig, E. On the origin of Judaism: A psychoanalytic approach. *The Psychoanalytic Study of Society*, 1976, *7*, 359-367.

Against Freud's view of the primal crime of father sacrifice, Lustig suggests that child sacrifice was much more typical of ancient pre-Judaic cultures. The Passover sacrifice is a substitute for sacrificing the firstborn, and this theme is found often in Judaic texts and rituals, though in muted form. The springtime festivals that marked the beginning of the year have been suppressed, except for Passover, and now the Judaic year starts in the fall. Circumcision, as practiced by Jews on the eighth day, is a condensation of puberty initiation and firstborn sacrifice, and thus is also a reminder of infanticide. Making the death of Jesus occur on Passover contributed to the success of Christian mythology of Jesus as the Messiah.

1330. Meissner, W.W. Jewish messianism and the cultic process. *The Psychoanalytic Study of Society*, 1990, *15*, 347-370.

Most of the article is devoted to a supposedly historical survey. The psychoanalytic part suggests that belief in the messiah is a compensation for narcissistic injuries. The messiah himself is a projection of idealized aspects of the believer's narcissistic introjective configuration. There is a paranoid process in a group through which objective weakness will be replaced by absolute power and enemies will be defeated.

1331. Merkur, D. The prophecies of Jeremiah. *American Imago*, 1985, *42*, 1-37.

While showing a high level of scholarship in the areas of both Biblical texts and psychoanalytic theory, this article chooses to treat Jeremiah as a real person, on the basis of Biblical texts alone. This leaves the reader puzzled, as speculations are offered about Jeremiah's superego, his father, etc.

1332. Merkur, D. Prophetic initiation in Israel and Judah. *Psychoanalytic Study of Society*, 1988, *12*, 37-67.

Starting with an exemplary scholarship in both Biblical literature and psychoanalysis, the author decides to treat Biblical figures as real personalities.

Thus he speculates about the prophet Ezekiel's unconscious conflicts and Oedipal wishes. This seems unwarranted, as Ezekiel remains a purely literary presence.

1333.   Peto, A. The demonic mother image in the Jewish religion. *Psychoanalysis and the Social Sciences*, 1958, *5*, 280-287.

It is suggested here that both positive and negative mother imagos were projected on the god of the ancient Israelites, while they themselves had also chosen a feminine identification and a passive homosexual solution to a collective Oedipal problem. To arrive at this idea, the author juxtaposes bits and pieces of ancient mythology, which he chooses to regard as history. Thus, he accepts the story of an exodus from Egypt, and a "desert period" in Israelite history, as proven facts. The overall result is confused and confusing.

1334.   Peto, A. The development of ethical monotheism. *The Psychoanalytic Study of Society*, 1960, *1*, 311-375.

This article attempts to reconstruct ancient Jewish history, while accepting the essentials of Biblical mythology as history. Treats the myth of the exodus from Egypt as history, as well as the wanderings in the desert. Suggests that there was a Judaic "desert religion", before the encounter with Canaanite religions in Palestine. At the same time, the author adopts the findings of Bible criticism and cites archeological data. Psychoanalytic interpretations of this history deal with the victory of the father-God over the mother-goddesses, through a passive homosexual attachment to the father.

1335.   Piers, G. The three superegos of the Western world: Psychoanalytic reflections of Judaism, Catholicism, and Calvinism. *Annual of Psychoanalysis*, 1983, *11*, 335-350.

An interesting, speculative discussion of the "collective" superegos in 3 historical traditions. Piers means by a collective superego the dominant world view in a culture. That of Judaism has been characterized by rationalism and an impersonal god, connected to compulsive behavior. Catholicism, with a personal Godhead, combining maternal and paternal qualities, is tied to submission without initiative. Calvinism, in which there is some return to Judaism, is tied to a striving for perfection.

1336.   Reik, T. *The Secret Self: Psychoanalytic Experiences In Life and Literature*. New York: Farrar, Straus and Young, 1953.

Interprets the struggle between Shylock and Antonio in *The Merchant of Venice* as a reflection of an older mythological motif: the contrast between Jehovah, the Old Testament God of vengeance, and Jesus, the young God of love. Shylock's intention of cutting off a pound of flesh represents castration. Shylock wanted to castrate the gentile (i.e. make him Jewish), but he is punished and forced to become a Christian.

1337.   Reik, T. The face of God. *Psychoanalysis*, 1955, *3*, (2), 3-26.

The traditional Jewish custom of wearing sidelocks, which seem to be growing out of the hat is regarded as an example of the "return of the repressed". Distinctive haircuts and hairdos have always been identity markings and symbols of religious commitment. Ancient Judaism specified a particular way of wearing the hair, but the historically recent custom of wearing hairlocks, typical of Orthodox Jews in Eastern Europe, is a return to the totemic religion, in which pre-historical Judaism enjoined its followers to resemble the ram.

1338.   Reik, T. The Shofar (Ram's Horn). In T. Reik, *Ritual: Psychoanalytic Studies*. New York: International Universities Press, 1958.

The Shofar is a relic of ancient totemic worship, which explains its special status in Judaism. The sound of the Shofar is assumed unconsciously to be the voice of God, similar to the roaring bull, which produces its awesome effect. Only the ram's horn is used, because it was the main totem of the ancient Israelites. This is a highly speculative piece, which is nevertheless well-argued.

1339.   Reik, T. Kol Nidre. In T. Reik, *Ritual: Psychoanalytic Studies*. New York: International Universities Press, 1958.

Here Reik tackles one of the greatest mysteries of Jewish liturgy: a prayer which no one really understands, and is nevertheless the most moving moment of the year for any believer. This is the prayer said as the Day of Atonement starts, which is then followed by 24 hours of praying and fasting. The interpretation offered here is a tour de force of psychoanalytic archeology. It is suggested that this unusual prayer, proclaiming the annulment of all vows, is an expression of the ancient original crime and its attendant totem feast. Rebellious impulses are expressed and then guilt and submission follow. The emotion involved, reflected also in the moving tune to which the prayer is pronounced, is a result of the unconscious process of blasphemy and return to faith.

1340.   Reik, T. A booth away from the house. *Psychoanalytic Review*, 1963, *50*, 167-186.

This is a chapter from Reik's *Pagan Rites in Judaism* (see 1341 below), and deals with the autumn Feast of Booths (Sukkot). On this occasion booths roofed with tree branches have to be built, and all males must eat and sleep there. Reik's hypothesis is that these booths are vestiges of prehistorical puberty rites, during which the young men had to live segregated in temporary housing within the forest. This is an exercise in "psychoanalytic archeology" inasmuch as Reik states "that the repressed in the history and prehistory of a people is really immortal and indelible" (p. 23). Beyond that, he offers a familiar interpretation of initiation rites as symbolic death and resurrection.

1341.   Reik, T. *Pagan Rites in Judaism*. New York: Farrar, Straus, 1963.

This work collects many examples of Jewish rituals and offers brilliant and original interpretations. The general theory is that all of these rituals, such as the blessing of the priests, menstrual taboos, and family rites are tied to a pre-historic, totemic Judaism. Totemism is also used to explain Jewish solidarity and family cohesion, maintained by totemic group boundaries, such as food taboos. The ceremony of the blessing of the priests is interpreted as representing an ancient totemic ritual in which the priests dressed in ram skins. The special way of holding the fingers is interpreted as representing the ram's hoofs. The prohibition against looking at the priests during the ceremony is a later development, dating from the period when the totem was replaced by an invisible god.

1342.   Roheim, G. Some aspects of Semitic monotheism. *Psychoanalysis and the Social Sciences*, 1955, *4*, 169-122.

Suggests that patriarchal elements in religion were overestimated by Freud, and maternal ties neglected. The primal crime (*Totem and Taboo*) in which the father was supposedly eaten, through identification with him and the wish to acquire his strength, might have been different. The mother was instead the sacrificial victim.

1343.   Rosenzweig, E.M. Some notes, historical and psychoanalytical on the people of Israel and the land of Israel with special reference to Deuteronomy. *American Imago*, 1940, *1*, 50-64.

This is a speculative article, mixing mythology with historical evidence. It seeks to prove that the cult of the Great Mother, so popular in ancient Palestine, was replaced among the ancient Israelites by the cult of the Land itself. Anxieties, rituals, and beliefs tied to the Mother Goddess, especially forms of sacrifice, became attached to the Land.

1344.   Rubenstein, R.L. *The Religious Imagination*. New York: Bobbs-Merrill, 1967.

This a an ambitious and impressive analysis of Talmudic legends which often express complexity and ambivalence. There is sometimes an identification with symbols of evil, which leads sages to describe Esau as a scholar. The analysis shows a surprising emphasis on pre-Oedipal motives. The main theme of legends, reflecting an unconscious concerns, is not Oedipal struggles and castration fears, but anxiety aroused by the mother. "Incorporation anxiety" is also a common fear, expressed in many legends.

1345.   Schlossman, H.H. God the father and his sons. *American Imago*, 1972, *8*, 35-51.

Claims that the familiar Biblical myths about the displacement of an older brother by a younger one really represent a pre-historical residue of practices in which the older son was sacrificed to maternal fertility goddesses. This existed in a matriarchal culture. The coming of patriarchy necessitated the creation of transition myths, which are what we find in the Bible.

1346.   Sillman, L.R. Monotheism and the sense of reality. *International Journal of Psychoanalysis*, 1949, *30*, 124-132.

Suggests that historical (i.e. Western) monotheism has been tied to an increasing sense of reality, which has brought about the rise of Western science and technology.

1347. Slochower, H. The Book of Job: The Hebrew myth of the Chosen God, its symbolism and psychoanalytic process. *International Record of Medicine*, 1958, *171*, 761-769.

This article offers the speculation that common interpretations of the book of Job, which emphasize its universalistic elements, are mistaken. Instead, it is viewed as a mythic representation of a uniquely Judaic history: the election of Yahweh as the chosen tribal god.

1348. Trachtenberg, M. Circumcision, crucifixion and anti-Semitism. *International Review of Psycho-Analysis*, 1989, *16*, 459-471.

This is a speculative article, with an historical introduction which confuses mythology and history. It connects circumcision to the crucifixion as both reflect castration. Among Jews, circumcision is a personal transition rite, and not just an image, as the crucifixion is to Christians. Anti-Semitism stems from a reaction to circumcision, which to Christians is a constant reminder of the crucifixion.

1349. Woolf, M. Prohibitions against the simultaneous consumption of milk and flesh in orthodox Jewish laws. *International Journal of Psychoanalysis*, 1945, *26*, 169-177.

The deepest impulse underlying this taboo is interpreted as related to the mother. Mixing meat with mother's milk means returning to the womb, and giving prominence to the mother, whose rights were obliterated by the father religion. Another impulse, not as deep, is the struggle against a relic from the pre-Judaic mother-goddess, Astrate, the goddess of fertility and love, whose cult was a target for hostility.

1350. Zeligs, D.F. A psychoanalytic note on the function of the Bible. *American Imago*, 1957, *14*, 57-60.

This brief note presents an ambitious and provocative hypothesis: that the Hebrew Bible can be read as one work, with one central motive. That motive, and that motif, is the Oedipal struggle. Like *Oedipus Rex* in Greek culture, the most important stage in our development is retold, but in the Hebrew Bible another denouement is offered. The Bible offers sublimation instead of acting-out and internalized morality instead of cruel fate.

For additional materials on this topic, see also 204, 206, 324, 335, 401, 415, 501, 502, 503, 507, 511, 512, 547, 551, 561, 567, 568, 610, 703, 704, 722, 725, 729, 804, 805, 820, 902, 1004, 1005, 1021, 1022, 1026, 1038, 1039, 1040, 1049, 1051, 1054, 1055, 1056, 1057, 1070, 1071, 1072, 1102, 1112, 1114, 1126, 1129, 1135, 1137, 1140, 1201, 1202, 1203, 1204, 1205, 1206, 1207, 1208, 1211, 1213, 1214, 1215, 1416, 1421, 1508, 1520, 1525, 2001, 2002, 2003, 2004.

And see Sections 4, 14, 15.

14

ANTI-SEMITISM

1401.   Ackerman, N.W. and Jahoda, M. *Anti-Semitism and Emotional Disorder: A Psychoanalytic Interpretation.* New York: Harper, 1950.

The phenomenon of anti-Semitism is always a combination of inner needs and social factors. Psychoanalysis can throw light on the former, and so forty cases of anti-Semites in analysis were selected for study. This group was marked by a variety of personality problems, as well as by unresolved Oedipal problems. Anti-Semitism is the externalized solution to inner weakness and conflict, through projection, denial, and rationalization. These explanations seem general and certainly are not sufficient to explain the phenomenon of anti-Semitism. Assuming that all anti-Semites suffer from psychopathology is clearly unwarranted.

1402.   Brenner, A.B. Some psychoanalytic speculations on anti-Semitism. *The Psychoanalytic Review*, 1948, *35*, 20-32.

Judaism is unique in denying any role to female consorts of the father-god. This must be very disturbing to non-Jews, who may view it as an indication of Jewish "maturity", as Jews no longer need a mother. Another possible unconscious reaction is that the Jews have solved the Oedipal situation by getting rid of their mother and (being circumcised) having taken her place. This explanation may be relevant to cases where the absence of a female deity in Judaism is indeed known to non-Jews.

1403.   Dubcovsky, S., de Schuldt, F. and Teper, E. Anti-Semitism: The magic reality conflict. *American Imago*, 1966, *23*, 132-141.

The development of Judaic monotheism was a denial of immortality and an attack on magical practices and funerary rites, which were the focus of neighboring religious traditions. This denial of omnipotence was the unconscious equivalent of the killing of the omnipotent father, and gave Jews the perennial role of scapegoats.

1404.   Fenichel, O. Psychoanalysis of antisemitism. *American Imago*, 1940, *1*, 24-39.

The Jew is an object that facilitates for the Christian a variety of projections, in a personality lacking complete identification and complete introjection. Aggression against Jesus Christ is then projected by Christians onto the Jews. On a social level, anti-Semitism presents a failure of the civilizing process.

1405.   Fenichel, O. Elements of a psychoanalytic theory of anti-Semitism. in *The Collected Papers of Otto Fenichel*. New York: Norton, 1954. (also in E. Simmel (ed.) *Anti-Semitism: A Social Disease*. New York: International Universities Press, 1946).

The Jew is the prototypical foreigner in Western culture, and thus attracts the projection of repressed impulses on the part of the majority. Circumcision gives rise to castration fears, and also to fantasies of revenge by Jews, making them into imaginary castrators. This combination of factors accounts for anti-Semitism.

1406.   Gilman, S. Anti-Semitism and the body in psychoanalysis. *Social Research*, 1990, *57*, 993-1017.

This scholarly and fascinating article reminds us that nineteenth-century racial theories, which emphasized indelible biological differences and the biological nature of Jews, were an important part of the cultural discourse of that period. Freud had to struggle with, and deny the idea of biological Jewishness in developing psychoanalysis. Gilman agrees with Freud and other analysts in regarding circumcision as a major preoccupation of both Jews and anti-Semites.

1407.   Glenn, J. Circumcision and anti-Semitism. *The Psychoanalytic Quarterly*, 1960, *29*, 395-399.

It is suggested here that the circumcised Jew is perceived as somebody who has been crippled, and triggers castration anxiety, because of the fantasy that he may want to avenge his maiming.

1408.   Grunberger, B. The anti-Semite and the Oedipal conflict. *International Journal of Psychoanalysis*, 1964, *45*, 380-385.

Anti-Semitic projections are pre-genital regressions, but Judaism also represents the worship of the Father and the victory of the Great Father over the pagan *Magna Mater*. Christianity represents the return of the Mother, and the Christian is the son who achieves unity with his Mother (as shown in pictorial representations of the virgin mother and her child). Worshipping the father not only arouses the Oedipal conflict, but expressed punitive submission to him. One solution is the splitting of the father imago into the bad father, who equals the Jew, and the good father, my own, represented also by God, country, and collective ideals. Loving the father means hating the Jews. The Jew represents the Oedipal father, both all-powerful and castrated.

1409.   Krapf, E. Shylock and Antonio: A psychoanalytic study of Shakespeare and anti-Semitism. *Psychoanalytic Review*, 1955, *42*, 113-130.

Following a discussion of Shakespeare's work and personality, and inspired by Melanie Klein's early work, the author suggests that anti-Semitism may be a defense against the castrating and phallic mother, which allows the anti-Semite to attack the Jew, simultaneously targeting the mother and the bad child who attacks her. The Jews are such a fitting target because they themselves are guilty of the same matricidal impulses.

1410. Loeblowitz-Lennard, H. The Jew as symbol. I. The ritual murder myth. *Psychoanalytic Quarterly*, 1947, *16*, 33-38.

Historically, the Jew is perceived as representing the transmitter, and the symbol, of moral force. To show that the Jew is immoral, and to destroy him, is the goal of the anti-Semite, because in this way the yoke of morality, imposed by the Jews, will be thrown off.

1411. Loeblowitz-Lennard, H. The Jew as symbol. II. Antisemitism and transference. *Psychoanalytic Quarterly*, 1947, *21*, 253-260.

Material from case studies is used to test the hypothesis that anti-Semitism can be understood as a case of transference dynamics. Anti-Semitic arguments, collective and individual, are judged to resemble childhood reactions to the father imago (Judaism appears to lack a mother imago). They are a negative transference reaction because they serve the impulse against societal authority, and against the resolution of the Oedipal situation and the creation of the superego.

1412. Loewenstein, R.M. The historical and cultural roots of antisemitism. *Psychoanalysis and The Social Sciences*, 1948, *1*, 313-356.

See 1413 below.

1413. Loewenstein, R.M. *Christians and Jews: A Psychoanalytic Study*. New York: International Universities Press, 1951.

The interpretation of anti-Semitism is based on an assumed projection of Oedipal conflicts. Exogamy rules, which preclude sexual contacts with outsiders, make them more desirable, and turn them into a representation of the Oedipal incestuous object. The outsider is the target of attraction, envy, guilt, and loathing. The teaching of the Church Fathers led to identifying the Jews with Satan, but this is a result of their identification with an evil god. The theological concept of the Jews, as developed in the Middle Ages, was based on their identification with two mythological figures: Cain and Judas. Historically, the Christian is bound to the Jew by both hatred and loyal indebtedness. There is a peculiar bond between them. The function of anti-Semitism has been to allow Christians to project their revolt against the mythological figure of Jesus, while keeping love to him at a conscious level.

1414. Ostow, M. A contribution to the study of Antisemitism. *Israel Journal of Psychiatry and Related Sciences*, 1983, *20*, 95-118.

A wide-ranging survey of history and psychological theories (including clinical cases), which offers original hypotheses about the dynamics of individual and social anti-Semitism. On an individual level, anti-Semitism may follow a disappointing personal attachment to Jews. On the social level, it is tied to group myths, such as the crucifixion.

1415.   Parkes, J. *Antisemitism.* Chicago: Quadrangle, 1969.

This work interprets anti-Semitism within the more general framework of prejudice. Prejudice is formed through the defense mechanisms of displacement, projection, and rationalization. Guilt is externalized, and internal balance kept.

1416.   Pederson, S. Unconscious motives in pro-Semitic attitudes. *Psychoanalytic Review,* 1951, *38,* 361-373.

The cultural mythology about Jews and Judaism makes them ideal objects for individual projections, both positive and negative. Based on 3 case studies, the author suggests that there are some generalities in these projections. When pro-Semitic attitudes are present, Jews are conceived of in fantasy as phallic mothers, possessing magical knowledge and vitality, and symbolize the magical omnipotent world of childhood.

1417.   Schick, A. The Jew as a sacrificial victim. *The Psychoanalytic Review,* 1971, *58,* 75-89.

This is a speculative essay on the symbolic role of Jews in Western history. Jews have always symbolized morality, because Judaism was the first religion to denounce and stop human sacrifice. Anti-Semitic movements are likely to appear during periods of cultural decline.

1418.   Schoenfeld, C.G. Psychoanalysis and antisemitism. *The Psychoanalytic Review,* 1966, *53,* 24-37.

Surveying and summarizing the psychoanalytic literature on anti-Semitism, the author offers some suggestions for prevention of this common prejudice. The psychoanalytic literature, starting with Freud, agrees on two generalizations. First, anti-Semitism, like other prejudices, is a symptom of an underlying conflict. Second, it is agreed that Judaism and actions by Jews may trigger anti-Semitism. On the non-Jewish side, anti-Semitism may result from projection of castration fears, intra-family hostility, and unconscious guilt. Judaism, with its rules of purity that separate Jews from non-Jews, discourages real intimacy between the two groups.

1419.   Simmel, E. Anti-Semitism and mass psychopathology. In E. Simmel (ed.) *Anti-Semitism: A Social Disease.* New York: International Universities Press, 1946.

Judaism represents the instinctual renunciation and the total spiritualization of religion, which creates strong opposition in non-Jews. Oral aggression is projected on Jews. The anti-Semitic Christian is in need of recreating the primitive totem animal, and accuses the Jew of the crime which he unconsciously commits when he eats the holy wafer. Anti-Semitic attitudes are likely to develop in individuals for whom the Jew represents their conflict with the father, and who suffer from a harsh and sadistic superego, leading occasionally to violent acting-out. Such attitudes are unlikely to appear in mature personalities, and so are tied to psychopathology.

1420.   Stein, H. The binding of the son: Psychoanalytic reflections on the symbiosis of anti-Semitism and anti-gentilism. *Psychoanalytic Quarterly*, 1977, *46*, 650-681.

This is an ambitious and speculative attempt to interpret Jewish history and Jewish identity vis-à-vis Christianity. Anti-Semitism and anti-gentilism are mirror images, part of the symbiosis between Jews and Christians. The Abraham-Isaac relationship is viewed as a paradigm for Jewish history, where victimhood and martyrdom are central.

1421.   Wangh, M. Anti-Semitism and Nazi anti-Semitism. *Psychoanalytic Quarterly*, 1963, *32*, 299-301.

This interesting article presents a general theory of prejudice. It defends against unconscious impulses, while at the same time expressing them. It has its roots in early infancy, when self-non-self separation has not been completely achieved. This incomplete separation leads to exaggerated love for self and hatred for others.

1421.   Weill, T.L. Anti-Semitism: Selected psychodynamic insights. *American Journal of Psychoanalysis*, 1981, *41*, 139-148.

This contribution is first an excellent literature survey, covering psychoanalytic ideas from Freud onward. The survey is non-critical and informative, and must be read by anyone interested in the psychoanalytic approach to anti-Semitism. The author's own suggestion is that anti-Semitism is the consequence of dynamics common to Jews and gentiles. Anti-semitism is tied to strong ambivalence about parents and anxiety and inferiority about sexual identity. There is a strange symbiosis between Jew and anti-Semite. The former accepts suffering as proof of his guilt and as a reinforcement of national identity. The latter needs the Jews to act out his aggression. Because of castration anxiety (circumcision), elitism, and the severe superego they represent, Jews are hard (or impossible) to love.

For additional materials on this topic, see also 412, 413, 414, 418, 419, 429, 723, 1053, 1205, 1324, 1336, 1348, 1525.

And see Sections 4, 13, 15.

15

CHRISTIANITY

1501.   Breuner, N.F. The cult of the Virgin Mary in Southern Italy and Spain. *Ethos*, 1992, *20*, 66-95.

Attempts to explain why Mary has remained a dominant figure in certain cultural-religious systems, while criticizing some of Carroll's (see 1502 below) explanations for the same phenomenon. The Mary cult is viewed as offering cultural solutions for cultural problems, specifically adapted to the needs of men and women. Marian devotion enables men to justify their control over women and lessens their fear of female sexuality. For women, Mary is an imaginary confidant and a source of comfort. She is a mother figure, and a model of femininity, as well as a source of power. This original interpretation can serve as a starting point for looking at women religious involvement in other cultures.

1502.   Carroll, M. P. *The Cult of the Virgin Mary: Psychological Origins*. Princeton: Princeton University Press, 1986.

This uniquely important study offers an Oedipus complex interpretation of the Marian cult, but goes beyond the classical formulation in two directions. One is that of family structure and dynamics, and the other one that of object relations theory. Carroll proposes that the emergence of a strong Marian cult requires first strongly repressed desire for the mother in her sons, and second, the lack of cohesive kin groups which transcend the nuclear family system and can serve as outlets for sexual energy. In his case studies, which concentrate on visions of the Virgin in France in the 19th century (Bernadette Soubirous in Lourdes, Catherine Laboure in Paris, and Maximin Giraud and Melanie Mathieu in La Salette), Carroll discusses early object relations and object representations, which have led to these particular hallucinatory experiences.

1503.   Carroll, M. P. *Catholic Cults and Devotions*. McGill-Queens Press, 1989.

Includes discussions of seven separate popular devotions, together with a discussion of the stigmata (1987) and a more general discussion of the splintering of Catholic devotions. Each ritual is described historically, and then psychoanalytic hypotheses are proposed and tested. The starting point is that all of these practices reflect infantile wishes and fantasies, especially having to do with anal eroticism, anal aggression, and castration. Specific theoretical ideas are taken from Freud and Melanie Klein. The overall result is refreshing and stimulating.

1504.   Carroll, M.P. Ernest Jones on Holy Communion: Refurbishing an early psychoanalytic insight. *Journal of Psychohistory*, 1991, *18*, 307-315.

Presents an early article by Ernest Jones (1910), which deals with the origins of Christian Communion, as well as mythology and art. In the article, Jones reported an association between fellatio and the act of receiving Holy Communion in a 39-yr-old female patient. It is suggested that the deemphasis of the Eucharistic wine in Christian myth and Christian art reflects the attempt to deny the imagery of oral sex, which could otherwise be activated by the experience of Communion.

1505.   Dundes, A. The hero pattern and the life of Jesus. *Colloquy 25*. The Center for Hermeneutical Studies. The Graduate Theological Union and the University of California, Berkeley, 1977.

This is a masterful performance, an analysis of the Jesus myth, using the resources of folklore studies and psychoanalysis, and looking at New Testament texts and other ancient texts. Dundes follows Rank and Raglan in the overall outline of the pattern, while differing from them on its interpretation. His interpretation is classical and Oedipal. However, it is pointed out that unlike other Oedipal heroes, Jesus does not kill his father, but rather submits to him. However, by becoming one with his father, Jesus achieves the Oedipal ideal of becoming his own begetter. The analysis here fits with other psychoanalytic contributions, but it is unique in its clarity.

1506.   Dundes, A. The hero pattern and the life of Jesus. *Psychoanalytic Study of Society*, 1981, *9*, 49-84.

An updated, revised version of 1505.

1507.   Edelheit, H. Crucifixion fantasies and their relation to the primal scene. *International Journal of Psychoanalysis*, 1974, *55*, 193-199.

Crucifixion fantasies and references in analytical and everyday materials are analyzed. It is suggested that the fantasy image of the crucified Jesus represents the image of the two parents locked in sexual intercourse and watched by the helpless child. A regressed version of the crucifixion represents the image of the nursing mother combined with the parents in intercourse, leading to the "Pieta" image.

1508.   Faur, J. De-authorization of the Law: Paul and the Oedipal model. In J.H. Smith and S.A. Handelman (eds.) *Psychoanalysis and Religion*. Baltimore and London: The Johns Hopkins University Press, 1990.

This chapter provides us first with a contribution to the psychoanalytic interpretation of religious myth in the classical fashion by presenting the Jesus myth as another Oedipal fable. It shows major Christian ideas to be Oedipal fantasies, accepted and used by believers. At the same time, Faur seems to be an apologist for his own religion, in this case Judaism.

1509. Feldman, A.B. Animal magnetism and the mother of Christian Science. *The Psychoanalytic Review*, 1963, *50*, 313-320.

Mary Baker Eddy has chosen the term Malicious Animal Magnetism, abbreviated to M.A.M., to designate evil. This article speculates about the possible origins of her ideas in childhood experiences, and concludes that she devalued femininity and maternity, while aspiring to phallic power.

1510. Freemantle, A. The Oedipal legend in Christian hagiology. *The Psychoanalytic Quarterly*, 1950, *19*, 408-409.

It turns out that the myth of Oedipus, by now familiar to students of psychoanalysis, has been attributed to the figure of Judas Iscariot of Christian mythology. Medieval legends claimed that Judas, following the exact outline of the Oedipal myth, killed his father and married his mother. It was after discovering his terrible crime that Judas, in this legend, meets Jesus and enters Christian mythology in search of absolution.

1511. Fromm, E. *The Dogma of Christ and Other Essays on Religion, Psychology and Culture*. London: Routledge, 1963. (New York: Holt, Rinehart and Winston, 1964, New York: Doubleday, 1966.)

Offers a Marxian-Freudian analysis of early Christianity. While this movement represented social revolt, on a psychological level it also represented an Oedipal rebellion and a victory over the father-god. Identification with a suffering man who was supposed to have become God was satisfying for the really suffering masses under Roman rule. Initially, there was hope for salvation in the political realm; when that turned out to be impossible, salvation became spiritual. Concurrently, maternal aspects of the deity became more central. The image of Jesus changed, as the young man Jesus was replaced by the baby in his mother's arms.

1512. Gordon, K.H. Jr. Religious prejudice in an eight year old boy. *The Psychoanalytic Quarterly*, 1965, *34*, 102-107.

The prejudice in this case refers to the expressed negative fantasies of a young boy in analysis about Christianity. The crucifixion myth is interpreted as castration. Jesus boasted about his mile long penis and was punished by God, who arranged to have the penis cut off on the cross. These fantasies are interpreted as a product of the boy's own wish to castrate his father. There are clear implications, neglected by the author, about the Oedipal message of Christian mythology.

1513. Jekels, L. The psychology of the festival of Christmas. *International Journal of Psychoanalysis*, 1936, *17*, 57-72.

An extremely lucid and interesting presentation of historical data and psychoanalytic hypotheses in an attempt to trace the origins of Christmas in the history of the Church in its early centuries. Christmas as a Christian holiday was created in the middle of the fourth century. It meant elevating the status of Jesus to equality with God the father. Why did it happen at that time ? The explanation is that the Church was responding to the wishes of the masses, who were experiencing hostility towards the superego God, who had caused their many sufferings, and wished to dethrone him. To this wish there was a strong guilt reaction, and the compromise solution was equality between Father and Son.

1514.   Jones, E. Psychoanalysis and the Christian religion. In E. Jones, *Essays in Applied Psychoanalysis*. Vol. 2. London: The Hogarth Press and the Institute of Psychoanalysis, 1951.

Christian mythology was capable of integrating the basic family system of mother, father, and son, while Judaism concentrated on the father, and other traditions focused only on the mother or the son. Later developments in Christianity in the direction of developing the Holy Ghost as the third person in the trinity are merely attempts to deny the son's incestuous desires, and the father's role in procreation. In Christian mythology, Jesus is the perfect son, adopting a passive position vis-à-vis his father (bearing the cross) and feminine characteristics in general (tenderness, forgiveness). Thus, his final identity is androgynous, and makes possible closeness to both parents. This imaginary ideal explains the attractiveness of Christianity.

1515.   Jones, E. The significance of Christmas. In E. Jones, *Essays in Applied Psychoanalysis*. Vol. 2. London: Hogarth Press, 1951.

The birth of the Christ child symbolizes rebirth. December 25 used to be celebrated as the winter solstice, the birthday of the sun, dead and born again. This was related to the custom of sacrificing a king during a totem feast. Christmas is thus tied to the crucifixion, in connecting birth to preceding death.

1516.   Lidz, T. and Rothenberg, A. Psychedelism: Dionysus reborn. *Psychiatry*, 1968, *31*, 116-125.

Drawing an analogy between the psychedelic fashions of the 1960s in the United States and ancient Greek cults, the authors offer a general sociological-historical analysis. Of psychoanalytic interest are their suggestions about similarities between the myth of Dionysus and the myth of Jesus, and the notion that the "psychedelic experience ... seems to be an internalization of the Christ symbol with its meanings of joy through suffering and absolution of sin through death" (p. 124).

1517.   Meissner, W.W. The origins of Christianity. *The Psychoanalytic Study of Society*, 1988, *13*, 28-62.

This speculative essay is based on a general acceptance of the framework of Christian mythology as history, although specific supernaturalist claims are never mentioned. Early Christianity is then interpreted as a "cult phenomenon", growing out of the paranoid process in individuals and groups.

1518. Moxon, C. A psychoanalytic study of the Christian creed. *International Journal of Psychoanalysis*, 1931, *2*, 54-70.

Reviews the Nicene Creed of Christianity as reflecting early childhood experiences. God is the beloved ego-ideal, with which the believers hope to be united. The belief in the virgin mother has clear Oedipal origins. While the author presents a secular view, he seems to regard Jesus as a historical figure.

1519. Philpott, S.J.F. Unconscious mechanisms in religion. *British Journal of Medical Psychology*, 1942, *19*, 292-312.

Most of this article, written during the dark days of World War II in Britain, may seem to us fifty years later hopelessly dated, theoretically incoherent (citing both Freud and Jung), and irrelevant. However, the persistent reader will be rewarded when reaching the final section, which contains a truly Freudian analysis of Christianity. It is suggested that the Jesus myth was a symbolic substitute for human sacrifice, and that firstborn sacrifice was justified by projecting it on God the Father. Christianity was also a popular movement, rising among the "common people," and it is they who will keep it alive, as they do with astrology and numerology.

1520. Sachs, H. At the gates of heaven. *American Imago*, 1947, *4*, 15-32.

Relying on a close examination, the original Greek texts of the New Testament (and accepting the events described there as historical), an analysis of the personality of the Apostle Paul and of the religion he created is attempted here. What Paul wanted to express in the Christianity he formulated was first and foremost a victory over death. Mystery religions of that historical period had all contained the idea of identification with a dying and resurrected god. This was celebrated in elaborate rituals of mourning and rejoicing. This tradition was connected by Paul to the Jewish notion of the Messiah. To become one with the resurrected son of God was the only way of overcoming death and sin. To achieve that, Paul developed two sacraments: baptism and Communion. At an unconscious level, he discovered a way of solving the internal conflict between ego and superego. By giving up the Law and uniting life and death through love, Paul made the superego into a life-giving and creative force.

1521. Schendler, D. Judas, Oedipus and various saints. *Psychoanalysis*, 1954, *2*, 41-46.

Popular versions of the Judas myth, which became associated with the Oedipus myth during the Middle Ages, are interpreted as ambiguous Christian solutions to the Oedipal situation.

1522. Schuster, D.B. The Holy Communion: An historical and psychoanalytic study. *The Bulletin of the Philadelphia Association for Psychoanalysis*, 1970, *20*, 223-236.

Pre-Christian totemistic feasts were focused on the devouring of the father. The Christian version is a clear departure from earlier traditions, because the sacrifice is voluntary and the victim is the son, rather than the father. This leads to a resolution of ambivalence about the father, the binding of homosexual drives, and the control of incest and murder.

1523.   Sereno, R. Some observations on the Santa Claus custom. *Psychiatry*, 1951, *14*, 387-396.

The highly original interpretation offered here is not strictly psychoanalytic and could be defined as "existential." It suggests that the gift-giving frenzy surrounding Christmas in modern Western cultures, characterized by crass commercialism, is an adult activity, with children as its innocent victims. Its true meaning is an attempt to escape the official religious message of the holiday. The Jesus story produces too much anxiety, and the preoccupation with presents and prices is a convenient escape.

1524.   Simo, J. On Christianity and the Oedipal winner. *Psychoanalytic Review*, 1983, *70*, 321-329.

Comparing the myth of Jesus with the prototypical Oedipus story, Jesus is defined as the "Oedipal winner", because of his reward in the form of eternal life in Heaven, at the side of his mother, following a symbolic father murder. Jesus murdered his father symbolically, through the Virgin Birth, which minimizes the role of the father, and the total marginality of Joseph, the earthly father. The original Oedipus was only punished, never rewarded. The model presented by Christian mythology encourages sublimation and socialized behavior, because it demonstrates that virtue is eventually rewarded. It also relieves guilt and self-destructive drives. This explains Christianity's historical success.

1525.   Tarachow, S. St. Paul and early Christianity: A Psychoanalytic and historical study. *Psychoanalysis and the Social Sciences*, 1955, *4*, 223-282.

This is a long and speculative discussion of the early history of Christianity. In addition to the historical part, which is not really psychoanalytic, it concludes with a number of interesting psychological hypotheses. Judaic monotheism is interpreted as a solution of the Oedipal problem by renunciation of mother worship and the renunciation of totemistic, aggressive, and magical practices in father worship (the author attempts to demonstrate a "return of the repressed" in Judaism, namely mother worship, but merely proves his ignorance of living Judaism). In Christianity there is a return to polytheism, with mother-son worship. The shift in Christianity from baptism to communion is a regression to oral aggression. Thus, the new religion was a compromise union between Judaism and its pagan neighbors. Later on, there was a transition from the androgynous Judaic solution to the latent passive homosexual solution of Catholicism. The origins of anti-Semitism are found in the challenge presented by Judaic renunciations, leading to Christian projections. The Jew is selected as scapegoat because God is Jewish.

1526.   Tarachow, S. Judas, the beloved executioner. *The Psychoanalytic Quarterly*, 1960, *29*, 528-554.

The figures of Jesus and Judas in Christian mythology are presented as tied by love and aggression. Jesus is a willing victim; Judas is invited to be the executioner. Anthropological and clinical evidence is presented to demonstrate killing in the service of the libido, and pre-Oedipal elements are emphasized. At some points the reader is left confused by the lack of boundaries between the discussion of mythology and of real individuals.

1527. Wayne, R. Prometheus and Christ. *Psychoanalysis and the Social Sciences*, 1951, *3*, 201-219.

The two mythological figures of Prometheus and Jesus are compared, through an examination of their representations in ancient literature. They are interpreted as two culture heroes in Oedipal rebellion, but while the first represents an open rebellion and underlying dependence, the second expresses manifest submission and latent rebellion. Both are said to represent compulsive character structures, formed around anal conflicts.

For additional materials on this topic, see also 215, 309, 312, 316, 324, 335, 415, 502, 503, 504, 511, 512, 524, 525, 527, 530, 531, 533, 534, 540, 542, 547, 551, 568, 605, 607, 608, 612, 613, 617, 618, 620, 621, 624, 628, 631, 708, 709, 715, 716, 718, 726, 806, 809, 821, 823, 903, 905, 906, 907, 909, 911, 914, 915, 916, 918, 919, 921, 922, 1007, 1027, 1029, 1032, 1033, 1038, 1051, 1052, 1053, 1054, 1057, 1064, 1065, 1066, 1102, 1103, 1113, 1118, 1125, 1134, 1136, 1140, 1141, 1145, 1205, 1313, 1323, 1329, 1330, 1335, 1336, 1346, 1348, 1408, 1413, 1414, 1417, 1420, 1421, 1903, 1906, 1910, 2004, 2008, 2102.

And see Sections 10, 11, 13.

16

ASIAN RELIGIONS
(BUDDHISM, HINDUISM)

1601. Berkley-Hill, O. The anal-erotic factor in the religion, philosophy, and character of the Hindus. *International Journal of Psychoanalysis*, 1921, *2*, 306-338.

Reviews the Hindu "pollution complex," including rituals and the caste system itself, with its class of "untouchables," and interprets them as a reflection of a cultural anal complex.

Asceticism, which begins in anal self-control, is central to Hinduism and the attitude of contempt towards the body viewed as filled with waste products is a major topic in religious literature. Ritualism is also tied to anality. The article gives much data about Hindu daily rituals, but parts of the discussion may be viewed by some today as reflecting prejudice.

1602. Chaudhuri, A.K.R. A psychoanalytic study of the Hindu mother goddess (Kali) concept. *American Imago*, 1956, *13*, 123-145.

The Hindu goddess Kali presented as a terrifying image of a cruel castrating woman, whose statues show her naked and adorned by flowing blood and severed human heads and hands, is interpreted as a projection of the infantile ambivalent image of the mother. Following Melanie Klein, it is suggested that the baby projects its own negative and positive impulses on its mother, thus creating a ambivalent fantasy. Kali contributes to the resolution of the Oedipal conflict by being a virgin, as well as stirring up castration fears. She is also a phallic woman, and castrates both fathers and sons.

1603. Kakar, S. *The Inner World: A Psycho-Analytic Study of Childhood and Society in India*. New York: Oxford University Press, 1978.

A psychoanalytic approach, inspired by Erikson and Kohut, is used to establish configurations of cultural symbols, as the author looks at Indian myths, doctrines, and social structure. The aim is to demonstrate how basic developmental themes turn into religious expressions, which in turn shape cultural and personal experience. A case study of the famous mystic Vivekananda is presented. Central religious ideas, such as dharma and karma, are shown to be tied to early experience.

1604.   Kakar, S. *Shamans, Mystics and Doctors: A Psychological Inquiry Into India and Its Healing Traditions.* Chicago: The University of Chicago Press, 1982.

This important and illuminating book gives us a psychoanalytic perspective on healers, patients, and seekers in India. Theories of healing and demonology, healing rituals, Tibetan shamans, tantric healing, and other practices are observed and interpreted not only according to psychoanalysis, but in relation to psychoanalytic theory and practices.

1605.   Kundu, G. Psychoanalysis of religion of an Indian primitive tribe. *Samiksa*, 1976, *30*, 47-54.

Discusses repression of sexuality as a major function of religion, focusing on the religion of the Bhumia Baiga, a traditional tribe in India. Acts directly or indirectly connected with sex are regarded as requiring purification through religious ceremonies. Men who control their sexual urge, are considered to be holy, whereas women are viewed as inferior in this respect because they cannot stop their menstrual cycle. At the same time, religious practices provide symbolic gratification of repressed sexual desires.

1606.   Kurtz, S.N. *All the Mothers Are One: Hindu India and the Cultural Reshaping of Psychoanalysis.* New York: Columbia University Press, 1992.

This is a report of fieldwork in India, together with a theoretical attempt at a new framework for psychoanalytic anthropology. The author discovered that his Hindu informants regarded all goddesses as the multiple identities of a single Mother Goddess. This cultural fact is interpreted as reflecting the early experiences of being raised by many "mothers" in the Indian family. These conditions of mothering create a cultural complex projected into religious beliefs.

1607.   Leach, E.R. Pulleyar and the Lord Buddha: An aspect of religious syncretism in Ceylon. *Psychoanalysis and the Psychoanalytic Review*, 1962, 49, 81-102.

This is a combined structuralist (following Levi-Strauss) and psychoanalytic analysis, which suggests that Pulleyar is the sexual counterpart to the ascetic Buddha. The former is tied to fertility, and the latter to salvation. Thus, a balance (and an imbalance) is maintained in the cultural system.

1608.   Newell, H.W. An interpretation of the Hindu worship of Siva Linga. *Bulletin of the Philadelphia Association for Psychoanalysis*, 1954, *4*, 82-86.

It is suggested that the Siva Linga, an object presenting a schematic penetration of a human vulva by a human penis, and which seems anatomically incorrect, may have other meanings. It may represent, more correctly as to anatomy, a bovine intercourse, or it may actually symbolize castration, as the organs are completely detached from the human body. It is the theme of castration that would put worshippers in the appropriate mood of humility.

1609. Paul, R.A. *The Tibetan Symbolic World: Psychoanalytic Explorations.* Chicago: University of Chicago Press, 1982.

This is a thorough dissection of a whole culture, based on anthropological fieldwork and classical psychoanalytic interpretations. Cultural systems, including religion, are viewed as attempts to resolve Oedipal problems, i.e. the struggles between older and younger males. Freud's reconstruction of such struggles in early human culture, as described in *Totem and Taboo*, is the starting point. Specific religious myths and rituals are analyzed within this framework. This volume may be heavy reading for those unfamiliar with the jargon of social anthropology, but it represents an important tradition in this field.

1610. Schnier, J. The Tibetan Lamaist ritual: Chod. *International Journal of Psychoanalysis*, 1957, *38*, 402-407.

Chod is a ritual dance performed by a single monk at night in a the mountains. He declares the suppression of passions and overcomes selfishness symbolically. At the end he offers his body to 'hungry demons' who devour him. This ritual has to be repeated hundreds of times during long wanderings, which take years. This cannibalistic fantasy is an expression of oral sadism. Following Melanie Klein, it is suggested that infancy fantasies about devouring the mother are projected on demons as a way of reducing guilt.

For additional materials on this topic, see also 525, 529, 539, 540, 566, 622, 718, 730, 814, 910, 912, 1030, 1130, 1131, 1322, 1701, 1902, 2102.

17

EGO PSYCHOLOGY AND RELIGION

1701.   Alexander, F. Buddhistic training as an artificial catatonia. *The Psychoanalytic Review*, 1931, *18*, 129-145.

Buddhist training in meditation is described as a withdrawal of libido from the world to be reinvested in the ego until an intra-uterine narcissism is achieved. It conquers the self, but loses the world. But Buddha, by starting a movement and not just withdrawing quietly from the world, has created conflicts and parricidal wishes in his followers, just like the case in other groups.

1702.   Beres, D. Psychoanalytic notes on the history of morality. *Journal of the American Psychoanalytic Association*, 1965, *13*, 3-37.

This is a long historical survey, without specific references to religion, but raising a general question of whether religion, as an external support for the superego, is necessary or even helpful. The author claims, based on his clinical experience, that religion actually discourages internalization, and thus leads to weak, dependent superegos, and no strong sense of morality. Thus, religious orthodoxy provides strong external supports to individuals with limited internal moral direction.

For additional materials on this topic, see also 312, 326, 347, 348, 501, 516, 523, 529, 541, 566, 569, 601, 618, 706, 707, 710, 721, 724, 731, 732, 735, 801, 802, 808, 812, 813, 1001, 1006, 1017, 1028, 1031, 1035, 1041, 1046, 1049, 1050, 1063, 1067, 1118, 1214, 1303, 1415, 1813.

And see Sections 5, 18.

18
OBJECT RELATIONS THEORY AND RELIGION

1801.   Almansi, R.J. On the persistence of very early memory traces in psychoanalysis, myth, and religion. *Journal of the American Psychoanalytic Association*, 1983, *31*, 391-421.

Presents observations on the persistence of early memory traces, and tentatively proposes that fragments of certain early perceptual experiences of the parental objects such as the sight of the face and the breast of the mother, the smiling or angry expression of the face, or the sight of the hands may occasionally be recoverable in the course of analysis. Some mythological figures and religious symbols may also traced back to similar motifs.

1802.   Brierley, M. Notes on Psychoanalysis and integrative living. *International Journal of Psycho-Analysis*, 1947, *28*, 57-105.

This is a wide-ranging discussion, most of which can be qualified as pro-religious or religious. Nevertheless, there are some striking observations about the importance of both Oedipal and pre-Oedipal elements in religious systems, as well as important references to the "depressive position", following Melanie Klein.

1803.   Brierly, M. *Trends in Psychoanalysis*. London: Hogarth, 1951.

Contains a sympathetic discussion of Christian mysticism, which translates the mystical experience into terms of positive personality growth.

1804.   Dare, C. An aspect of the ego psychology of religion: a comment on Dr. Guntrip's paper. *British Journal of Medical Psychology*, 1969, *42*, 335-340.

This is a response to Guntrip's paper (see 1807 below), which suggests that an apprehension of the world as incomplete is an innate attribute of the ego. Then, this incompleteness is dealt with through art, science, and religion. The author rejects the notion of neurotic religion, which cannot be verified, and the notion that the "non-neurotic" are always religious.

1805.   Finn, M. and Gartner, J. (eds.) *Object Relations Theory and Religion: Clinical Applications*. Westport, CT; Greenwood Press, 1992.

An interesting collection of ten chapters and an afterword, consisting mostly of clinical case studies, and reflecting the thinking of practitioners. A few chapters are more theoretical and contain interesting original ideas, but several of the contributions are marred by apologetics.

1806.   Guntrip, H. *Personality Structure and Human Interaction.* New York: International Universities Press, 1961.

Guntrip expresses here a general apologetic position, based on respect for religion: "Naturally, religion, dealing as it does with the emotional needs of human beings as persons, will be more liable to adulteration by the importation of infantile dependence into its motivation than will science. Nevertheless, man has shown an age old desire for the emotional security that would result from the knowledge that our life as 'persons' arises out of and remains rooted in a fundamentally 'personal' element in the structure of the universe. It is the task of philosopher and theologian to show whether that is realistic, but he would be a bold, foolish man who would insist that is in itself a neurotic wish" (p. 383). Other representative quotations:" Religion, like psycho-analysis, is a search for a psycho-therapy for the emotional and personal ills of human beings even if the method of approach is different" (p. 45). "Religious experience is so very much an expression of human nature as rooted in the primary need for good personal relationship ..." (p. 255). "... religion is about the human being's innate need to find good object-relationship in which to live his life" (p. 257).

1807.   Guntrip, H.J.S. Religion in relation to personal integration. *British Journal of Medical Psychology,* 1969, *42,* 323-333.

This article is first an impassioned defense of religion, but then offers some psychological hypotheses about its origins. It is assumed that persons have a basic need for others, rather than "instincts", and that we all possess internal objects. Claims that "religious experience" is the same kind of "stuff" as human "personal relations experience", and that there is "neurotic" and "non-neurotic" religion. However, this does not seem to go beyond a projection theory of religion. We need to relate to the universe and so we do that by projecting internal objects onto the universe.

1808.   Klein, M. *Narrative of a Child Analysis.* London: Hogarth Press, 1961.

Includes references to Richard's (10 years old) religious fantasies. He believed in a God that could punish him through thunder and lightning, and had similar fantasies about the bad, omnipotent father.

1809.   Milner, M. *The Suppressed Madness of Sane Men: Forty-Four Years of Exploring Psychoanalysis.* London: Routledge, 1987.

Contains several fascinating discussions of religious experiences and religious art, interpreted in terms representing both classical Freudian views and object-relations approaches. Includes useful references to several other psychoanalytic writings.

1810.   Rizzuto, A.M. Object relations and the formation of the image of God. *British Journal of Medical Psychology*, 1974, *47*, 83-99.

Reports two clinical case studies of individuals in treatment in which the God symbol was closely connected to the father image. The suggested interpretation is that the elements forming the God image originate in early childhood object representations. This is an earlier version of 1811.

1811.   Rizzuto, A.M. *The Birth of the Living God.* Chicago: University of Chicago Press, 1979.

The formations and transformation of God representations, which may be construed as "transitional objects", because they are presented to the young child by the surrounding culture as part of objective reality. In search of developmental laws that govern this formation, it has been found that it follows ego processes of defense and adaptation, as well as all meaningful interpersonal relations. Thus, the image of God is created not only through the projection of early father-child relations, but also through the impact of other early relationships, such as mother-son, daughter-father, daughter-mother. Still, father projection is found to be highly relevant to the development of religious beliefs. The author claims that there is no relationship between religious faith and personal maturity.

This book contains a thorough survey of Freud's ideas and brilliant summaries of the material, together with a review of object relations ideas and clinical observations. The theoretical part is a must for any student of classical psychoanalysis.

1812.   Ross, M.E. and Ross, C.L. Mothers, infants, and the psychoanalytic study of ritual. *Signs*, 1983, *9*, 26-39.

Suggests that when object relations theory is added to the range of psychoanalytic interpretations used, the influence of the mother and pre-Oedipal factors can be recognized in rituals. The Eucharist is used as an example.

1813.   Ross, N. Beyond "The Future of an Illusion". *Journal of the Hillside Hospital*, 1968, *17*, 259-276.

An extremely important theoretical discussion. While criticizing Freud's view that religion is a universal neurosis, the author proposes an object relations theory of the origins of religion.

"The need for religious faith represents the dread of object loss... religious phenomena represent projections of the need for the sustained, eternal existence of an immutably protective loving object--such projections also contain the most archaically ambivalent attitudes toward the earliest object; maneuvers of various obsessive, propitiatory...types all serve the purpose of trying to retain the lost object... the loss of ego boundaries one observes in psychopathological states ... based on an archaic ego state, but that the same phenomenon as experienced by religious individuals represents a regression in the service of the ego, which has a salutary effect on the capacity to retain object relations...."

1814.   Winnicott, D.W. *The Maturational Process and the Facilitating Environment.* New York: International Universities Press, 1965.

This is a general presentation of one variety of the British object-relations theory, as it applies to early development. It is a classical statement, which has stimulated much later work, and is now part of the canon of modern psychoanalysis. Contains several ideas which can be applied to religion, and several specific references to the "transitional stage" and "transitional objects", as ways of understanding religion. In addition, there is a original conceptualization of mystical states.

For additional materials on this topic, see also 224, 337, 347, 415, 517, 524, 525, 530, 535, 538, 539, 543, 545, 546, 559, 564, 568, 602, 607, 608, 618, 626, 631, 701, 706, 709, 713, 714, 719, 720, 721, 722, 728, 729, 730, 732, 736, 802, 803, 804, 807, 811, 814, 815, 816, 817, 819, 821, 822, 905, 912, 918, 1016, 1046, 1058, 1067, 1069, 1120, 1135, 1210, 1342, 1408, 1409, 1421, 1501, 1511, 1602, 1610, 1910, 1913, 1922, 2007, 2009.

And see Sections 6, 17, 19, 20, 21

19

ACADEMIC STUDIES OF PSYCHOANALYTIC HYPOTHESES

1901. Argyle, M. and Beit-Hallahmi, B. *The Social Psychology of Religion*. London: Routledge and Kegan Paul, 1975.

This book reviews the research literature in academic psychology and the social sciences, as it relates to religion. Contains several discussions of psychoanalytic hypotheses and the evidence supporting them, specifically the father projection hypothesis and the superego projection hypothesis. On the whole concludes that there is significant support for psychoanalytic theorizing about religion in 20th century social science literature.

1902. Bose, U. A psychological approach to the origin of religion and the development of the concepts of god and ghost in children. *Samiksa*, 1948, 2, 25-64.

This is a questionnaire survey unique for its population, and aiming to assess Indian children's fantasies about "Ghost" (presumably the "devil") and about God. The results are interpreted as supporting the Freudian theory of the formation of deity and devil images.

1903. Deconchy, J.P. God and parental images: The masculine and feminine in religious free associations. In A. Godin (ed.) *From Cry to Word*. Brussels: Lumen-Vitae, 1968.

In a study of 4660 French Catholic children, parental references to God were found to increase in both girls and boys between the ages of 9 and 15. The image of God in boys was more often connected to the maternal image of the Virgin Mary and less often to the image of Jesus, while the opposite was true for girls.

1904. Eisenman, R., Bernard, J.L., and Hannon, J.E. Benevolence, potency and God: A semantic differential study of the Rorschach. *Perceptual and Motor Skills*, 1966, 22, 75-78.

Twenty six female respondents rank-ordered the Rorschach cards according to the degree that they symbolized God. Then the cards were rated on Benevolence and Potency. God was seen as Benevolent, more than Potent. There was an order effect, with cards VII-X being rated as closer to symbolizing God.

1905.   Godin, A. and Hallez, M. Parental images and divine paternity. In A. Godin (ed.) *From Religious Experience to Religious Attitude*. Brussels: Lumen Vitae, 1964.

In a study of 30 Belgian men and 40 Belgian women, significant correlations were found between the image of the parents and the image of God. These correlations reflected preferences for parents, but the highest correlations were found for individuals reporting no preferences for either parent.

1906.   Hood, R.W., Jr., Morris, R.J., Watson, P.J. Male commitment to the cult of the Virgin Mary and the passion of Christ as a function of early maternal bonding. *International Journal for the Psychology of Religion*. 1991, *1*, 221-231.

M. P. Carroll's (see 1502) claims about the origin of the Catholic cult of the Virgin Mary are tested empirically. This study looked at the connection between early maternal bonding and preferences for religious images. Seventy-one non-Catholic males, selected for religious commitment, evaluated independently operationalized crucifixes and representations of the Virgin Mary. As predicted, an operational interactive measure of early maternal care and protection, indicative of repression, and the Parental Bonding Instrument, best predicted selecting both a suffering Christ and an erotic/nurturing Virgin Mary.

1907.   Lambert, W.W., Triandis, H.M. and Wolf, M. Some correlates of beliefs in the malevolence and benevolence of supernatural beings: A Cross societal study. *Journal of Abnormal and Social Psychology*, 1959, *57*, 162-168.

Beliefs in malevolent beings was found to be correlated with cruel socialization practices, and early experience was found to be projected onto the cosmos, in agreement with psychoanalytic predictions.

1908.   Larsen, L. and Knapp, R.H. Sex differences in symbolic conceptions of the deity. *Journal of Projective Techniques and Personality Assessment*, 1964, *28*, 303-306.

The deity image as rated by females was more benevolent, while males rated it as more punitive. This is interpreted as supporting the Oedipal origins of the deity image.

1909.   Lowe, W.L. Psychodynamics in religious delusions and hallucinations. *American Journal of Psychotherapy*, 1953, *7*, 454-462.

Eleven patients with religious delusions were studied by means of interviews, psychological tests, and a Religious Projection Test. It was found that the hallucinations, mostly auditory, were used to reinforce delusional beliefs. In their pre-morbid histories all patients showed a pattern of extreme dependence on the father.

1910.   McKeown, B.F. Identification and projection in religious belief: A Q-technique study of psychoanalytic theory. *Psychoanalysis and Contemporary Science*, 1976, *5*, 479-509.

An intensive study of three individuals by means of the Q-technique, a rating system in which an object is judged on fifty adjectives, and then ratings are correlated. The findings revealed an internal structure of identification, projection, and displacement. The most important finding is that the respondents identified with Jesus Christ, rather than with God. The image of God was too abstract, and negatively perceived.

1911. Nelson, M.O. The concept of God and feelings towards parents. *Journal of Individual Psychology*, 1971, *27*, 46-49.

This study failed to support Freud's idea about God as father-projection and found support for Adler's theory, which regarded God as a concretization of human ideas about perfection and greatness. There was a correlation between God images and parent preference -- those who preferred father saw God in his image and vice versa. Males saw God as father and vice versa.

1912. Nelson, M.O. and Jones, E.M. An application of the Q-technique to the study of religious concepts. *Psychological Reports*, 1957, *3*, 293-297.

A comparison of God images with parental images showed that the similarity to mother was greater, and all correlations were higher for females. The highest correlation was, for females, that of the images of father and Jesus, .543.

1913. Potvin, R.H. Adolescent God images. *Review of Religious Research*, 1977, *19*, 43-53.

This report is based on responses of 501 males and females aged 13-18, a representative sample of the United States population. The main finding is that God is perceived as both loving and punishing by the largest group (almost 50%). Another finding is that parental influence and formal religious education are the best predictors of belief in God. There is also a connection between the perception of parents as controlling as the perception of God as punishing. The finding can clearly be viewed as supporting a projection interpretation of religion, as well as indicating the importance of socialization.

1914. Siegman, A.W. An empirical investigation of the psychoanalytic theory of religious behavior. *Journal for the Scientific Study of Religion*, 1961, *1*, 74-78.

In a study of 85 Israeli students and 79 American students, low correlations were found for father-god (the highest was .35). Some support was found for the hypothesis that feelings and concepts tied to "God" are correlated with the same about one's father.

1915. Spiro, M.E. and D'Andrade, R.G. A cross-cultural study of some supernatural beliefs. *American Anthropologist*, 1960, *60*, 456-466.

If religion is a projection, and religions are cultural projective systems, then there should be a connection between the characteristic experiences in a culture and its projective system. This hypothesis is tested by using anthropological data from numerous cultures. The findings indicate a correlation between the treatment of children (i.e. early childhood experiences and memories) in a given culture, and the presumed benevolence or malevolence of deities in the same culture.

1916. Strunk, O. Perceived relationships between parental and deity concepts. *Psychological Newsletter*, 1959, *10*, 222-226.

In a study of twenty Protestant US students (males) using the Q-technique, higher correlations between God images and maternal images, as compared to paternal images, were found.

1917. Tamayo, A, and Desjardines, L. Belief systems and conceptual images of parents and God. *Journal of Psychology*, 1976, *92*, 131-140.

This cross-cultural study showed clear interactions between the parental object projected on the deity image, and culture. In Zaire, Indonesia, and Philippines, God was more similar to father. In the USA, Belgium, and Columbia, both parents were projected.

1918. Tamayo, A. and Dugas, A. Conceptual representations of mother, father, and god, according to sex and field of study. *Journal of Psychology*, 1977, *97*, 74-84

This study of 251 French Canadian university students showed that the image of the mother was most appropriate to describe God.

1919. Ullman, C. Cognitive and emotional antecedents of religious conversion. *Journal of Personality and Social Psychology*, 1982, *43*, 183-192.

This is a comparative study of 40 converts (to Catholicism, Orthodox Judaism, ISKCON, and Bahaism) and a control group of 30 non-converts (members of the same groups) by means of intensive interviews. The aim was to test the psychoanalytic explanation for conversion, which emphasizes problems in the relationship with one's father, with the "cognitive quest" hypothesis. Almost one third of the converts reported the loss of their fathers by death or divorce before age 10. About half of them reported unsatisfactory and stressful relations with their fathers. Thus, the psychoanalytic explanation was clearly supported.

1920. Vergote, A. and Tamayo, A. *The Parental Figures and the Representation of God*. The Hague: Mouton Publishers, 1981.

This extensive study of the correlations between parental and deity images showed that the representation of God includes both paternal and maternal attributes. The projection, however, is positive, and not ambivalent, which may be regarded as contradicting psychoanalytic predictions. Among schizophrenics and delinquents the image of God was found to be more maternal.

1921. Vergote, A., Tamayo, A. Pasquali, L., Pattyn, M. and Custers, A. Concept of God and parental images. *Journal for the Scientific Study of Religion*, 1969, *8*, 79-87.

In a study of 180 US students using adjective ratings, clear, positive correlations were found between parental images and deity image. The correlations found were, for father-god, .70, and for mother-god, .37.

1922. Whiting, J.W.M. Totem and taboo: A re-evaluation. *Science and Psychoanalysis*, 1960, *3*, 150-155.

Tests Freud's notion of the correlation between Oedipal conflicts and totemism by looking at anthropological reports of sleeping arrangements for babies and mothers and the prevalence of totemism in 57 societies. According to Whiting's version of the Freudian hypothesis, totemism will be prevalent in societies with a nuclear family, that is, the two parents sleeping together, with the child excluded. Of 37 cultures with the nuclear family pattern, only 9 had totemism, while of 20 in which mother and child sleep together, 14 have totemism. Mother-child relations in the latter group are bound to cause ambivalence and hostility, because the happy symbiosis ends with a rude separation (usually around age 3). The results do not support an interpretation of the totem as a father projection, and Whiting proposes that it may be actually a mother projection, with cannibalistic fantasies directed at her.

For additional materials on this topic, see also 302, 502, 801, 804, 807, 822, 1034, 1303, 2101.

20

MOTHER-WORSHIP

2001. Barag, G. The mother in the religious concepts of Judaism. *American Imago*, 1946, *4*, 32-53.

A great deal of material is covered here, mostly in the style of "psychoanalytic archeology," regarding goddess worship and feminine symbols in Judaism. In addition to the historical evidence, most of it dated and open to differing interpretations, there are some more general, and important, insights. One is the identification of the Judaic community with the divine mother and on the other hand, its passive-homosexual relation to the father. Another is the tendency to merge mother and father into a single deity. This is considered to be the essence of Judaic monotheism.

2002. Barag, G. Question of Jewish monotheism. *American Imago*, 1947, *4*, 8-25.

This article includes some speculation over bits and pieces of historical data, but also some important psychological hypotheses. Monotheism is viewed as based on the turning towards the father and away from the mother, and its aim is really overcoming love for the mother, through the Father imago which unites maternal and paternal features. It creates in its followers narcissism and fanaticism, the latter reminiscent of paranoia, which is tied to homosexual wishes. This explains the psychological satisfaction available to believers. The worship of the mother goddess has been abandoned in Jewish monotheism, but the mother aspect is constituent of the image of the father God, who is actually bisexual. The Torah, the Law, so central to Judaism, is also viewed as feminine.

2003. Brenner, A.B. The great mother goddess: puberty initiation rites and the covenant of Abraham. *The Psychoanalytic Review*, 1950, *37*, 320-340.

This is a contribution to "psychoanalytic archeology", taking as its starting point the primal horde crime of *Totem and Taboo*, and then searching for remnants of Great Mother worship in Judaism. Following Reik's interpretations of initiation rites, the Judaic custom of circumcision is interpreted as separating the infant from his mother and establishing the authority of the father, denying any vestiges of

Mother Goddess worship. Thus, it is the end point in the struggle to submerge the latter.

2004.   Halpern, S. The man who forgot he crucified Jesus: An exegesis of Anatole France's "Procurator of Judea". *Psychoanalytic Review,* 1964-65, *51,* 597-611.

This interpretation (mixing mythology and history) of a modern story inspired by Christian myth and Roman history contains some striking insights about Judaic traditions and about the dynamics of Christian ideals. The cross is interpreted as a mother symbol, with the son nailed with his back to it in order to avoid incest. This is tied to the misogyny in the New Testament, and to conscious and unconscious concerns about the mother and the Mother Goddess.

2005.   Kohen, M. The Venus of Willendorf. *American Imago,* 1946, *3,* 49-60.

The statuette of a pre-historical fertility goddess, whose face is covered, is the occasion for a discussion of the ambivalence towards the mother, which is projected on goddesses and mortals alike. Men view their mothers as castrating and castrated, while still desiring them. They would defend themselves by either projecting a totally positive image or by expressing ambivalence through the symbol of the covered face.

2006.   Roheim, G. Aphrodyte, or the woman with a penis (comparative mythology). *Psychoanalytic Quarterly,* 1945, *14,* 350-390.

This long article briefly discusses various goddesses only at its beginning and its ending, but offers many stimulating ideas for students of religion and mythology. It may be considered a masterpiece, as well as a test case, of classical psychoanalytic interpretation. It offers explanations along the lines of castration fears but also suggests important ties between pre-genital experiences and Oedipal sentiments. Roheim collects an enormous number of anecdotes from European folklore, mythology, and African initiation rites, specifically genital mutilations, which all center on the notion of the phallic mother. The use of clinical case materials to illustrate male fears of female sexuality and the persistence of pre-genital ideas in adult women is especially illuminating.

2007.   Roheim, G. Saint Agatha and the Tuesday woman. *International Journal of Psychoanalysis,* 1946, *27,* 119-126.

Interprets folk traditions found all over Europe as taboos expressing natural ambivalence about the superego and its dictates. The origins of the superego, according to Roheim, are found in "aggression turned against the object (mother) and then turned in against the Ego". Breaking the taboo expresses aggression against the mother-imago or supernatural being.

2008.   Ware, J.G. Greater still is Diana of the Ephesians. *American Imago,* 1962, *19,* 253-275.

Starting with Freud's earlier observations about the persistence of the Mother-Goddess worship under various guises, here we have an extended and erudite treatment of the same topic. The historical survey is scholarly and sweeping, from pre-historic times to the dogma of the Assumption declared by the Roman Catholic Church in 1950. This is interspersed with psychoanalytic explanations. The most important contribution is the developmental distinction between father god worship and mother goddess worship. It is proposed that the dynamics of the former occur relatively late, and are based on superego introjects. The resulting form of religion is likely to be rationalistic and intellectualized. The latter derives its impetus from the first year of life, and the resulting religion is personal, emotional, and ecstatic, as individuals seek to find union with the early mother imago. The discussion seems timely, as Mariolatry has lost little of its force.

2009. Weigert-Vowinkel, E. The cult and mythology of the Magna Mater from the standpoint of psychoanalysis. *Psychiatry*, 1938, *1*, 347-378.

Surveying the historical evidence on many ancient cults, the conclusion is that most religions are failed attempts to resolve the father-son conflict, but when we turn to mother-religions, things don't look much better. Mother worship brings up both the inevitable competition with the father and early childhood fears about separation from the mother. The Great Mother arouses much ambivalence as she is both "... a familiar attraction and a strange danger". The Phrygian-Roman cult of Cybele required self-castration (priestly celibacy may derive from that). Pre-historic mother worship in the form of fertility rites is tied to human sacrifice, and (following Melanie Klein) interpreted as "the result of an unbroken mother tie, which increases the danger of castration, the result of a general manic-depressive disposition".

For additional materials on this topic, see also 539, 542, 561, 564, 568, 1002, 1022, 1138, 1305, 1312, 1318, 1323, 1333, 1334, 1342, 1343, 1344, 1345, 1349, 1408, 1502, 1511, 1906, 1910, 1916, 1917, 1921, 1922.

And see Sections 5, 18, 20.

21

FATHER PROJECTION

2101.   Beit-Hallahmi, B. and Argyle, M. God as a father projection: The theory and the evidence. *British Journal of Medical Psychology*, 1975, *48*, 71-75.

Surveys eleven academic studies that have attempted to assess the similarity between individual images of the parents and the perceived image of God. Concludes that while most of the findings do not support a straightforward paternal projection hypothesis, they do support a parental projection explanation, thus leading to viewing religion as a projective system.

2102.   Bellah, R.N. Father and son in Christianity and Confucianism. *The Psychoanalytic Review*, 1965, *52*, 92-114.

Suggests that the projection hypothesis, and the Oedipal hypothesis, may have their limitations in the sense that not only are human families projected heavenward, but divine families may affect earthly practices. Even the outcome of the Oedipal situation may be affected by religious symbolization.

2103.   Cronin, H.J. Psychoanalytic sources of religious conflicts. *Medical Record*, 1934, *139*, 32-44.

Two kinds of observations are offered here. First, historical observations on the decline of religion, and the subsequent decline in the importance of religion in deep intrapsychic conflict. The author states that until the Middle Ages people were ready to kill each other over theological questions, but such times are long gone. Second, clinical cases, which are interpreted as showing that conscious attitudes towards religion are always unconscious projections of attitudes towards parental authority.

2104.   Ostow, M. The need to believe: Persistent religious behavior in non-believers. *International Record of Medicine and General Practice Clinics*, 1955, 168, 798-802.

An insightful discussion of the vestiges of religious belief and behavior, based on clinical cases of declared non-believers, who are still in imaginary and behavioral dialogue with deities. It is shown that in all cases these conflicts have to do with unresolved issues relating to one's father. Concludes that the need to believe "... is an autochthonous psychic need to serve and to believe in a paternal figure". This is an important application of the classical model of father-projection.

For additional materials on this topic, see also 415, 503, 542, 567, 807, 1024, 1054, 1057, 1305, 1306, 1323, 1408, 1512, 1810, 1903, 1904, 1905, 1907, 1908, 1909, 1910, 1911, 1912, 1913, 1914, 1915, 1916, 1917, 1918, 1919, 1920, 1922.

And see Sections 5, 13, 15, 20

AUTHOR INDEX

Daly, C.D., 1202
D'Andrade, R.G., 1915
Dare, C., 1804
Day, F., 307
Deconchy, J.P., 1903
Deikman, A.J., 707
de Monchy, S.J.R., 1016
de Schuldt, F., 1403
Desjardines, L., 1917
Desmonde, W.H., 204, 514, 1104, 1105, 1106
Deutsch, H., 1017
Devereux, G., 536, 609
DeVos, G., 1107
Diller, J.V., 409
Dubcovsky, S., 1403
Duff, I.F.G., 908
Dugas, A., 1918
Dundes, A., 1018, 1019, 1108, 1109, 1505, 1506

Edelheit, H., 1020, 1507
Eder, M.D., 1311, 1001
Eisenbud, J., 610
Eisenman, R., 1904
Eisler, E.R., 308
Eissler, K.R., 309
Ekstein, R.A., 708
Endleman, R., 515
Erikson, E.H. 516, 611, 909, 910, 1110, 1111
Evans, W.N., 809

Fairbairn, W.R.D., 709
Falk, A., 410
Farrell, B.A., 310, 311
Faur, J., 1508
Feldman, A., 517
Feldman, A.A., 1312, 1313
Feldman, A.B., 205, 518, 1314, 1509
Fenichel, O., 1404, 1405
Ferenzi, S., 519
Finn, M., 1805
Fisher, D.J., 711
Flugel, J.C., 312
Fodor, A., 207, 1022, 1317, 1318, 1319
Fodor, N., 1319
Forsyth, D.W., 1118
Fortes, M., 208
Fortune, R.F., 1023
Fox, R., 520
Fraiberg, L., 1113
Fraiberg, S., 1113
Freehof, S.W., 1320

Freeman, D., 209, 521
Freeman, T., 522
Freemantle, A., 1510
Frieden, K., 411
Fromm, E., 1511

Garma, A., 1114
Gartner, J., 1805
Gay, P., 313
Gay, V.P., 210, 523, 911, 1115, 1116
Gilbert, A.L., 612
Gilman, S., 412, 1406
Girard, R., 1117
Glenn, J., 1407
Godin, A., 1905
Goldfrank, E.S., 1024
Goldman, H.E., 1025
Gonen, J. Y., 1026
Goodich, M., 613
Gordon, K.H. Jr, 1512
Graber, R.B., 1027, 1118
Graves, R., 1321
Greenacre, P., 712
Greenberg, D., 1119
Greene, J.C., 614
Grinberg, L., 1322
Grinstein, A. 104, 1028
Grollman, E.A. 413, 1323
Groot, A.D. de, 1029
Groves, E. R., 314
Grunberger, B., 1408
Guntrip, H.J.S., 1806, 1807

Hallez, M., 1905
Halpern, S., 2004
Hannon, J.E., 1904
Harrison, I.B., 713, 714
Hartocolis, P., 715, 716
Heimbrock, H.G., 315, 1120
Henderson, J., 524
Hitschmann, E., 810, 913
Hofling, C.E., 1030
Homans, P., 316, 317, 414
Hood, R.W., Jr, 717, 1906
Hopkins, P., 718
Horton, P.C., 719, 720
Huckel, H., 1031
Hutch, R.A., 525
Hyman, S.E., 318

Ingham, J.M., 415

TITLE INDEX

SUBJECT INDEX

adolescence 719, 803, 808, 812, 816, 817
Amish, 1118
anality, 508, 609, 1103, 1109, 1601
ancient Egypt. *See* Egypt
ancient Greece
ancient religions, 522, 564, 1051, 1052, 1104,
    1105, 1135, 1209, 1212, 1303, 1312,
    1313, 1317, 1318, 1328, 1341, 2009
"animal magnetism", 1509
animism 551, 552, 553, 554
anthropology, 208, 209, 213, 214, 218, 314,
    319, 320, 323, 324, 325, 338, 344, 415,
    520, 521, 529, 532, 536, 543, 549, 552,
    553, 554, 555, 565, 566, 616, 622, 805,
    1003, 1008, 1009, 1015, 1024, 1034,
    1048, 1064, 1101, 1108, 1501, 1606,
    1607, 1609, 1907, 1915, 1922
anti-Semitism. *See* Section 14
Apache, 1008
apocalypse, 624, 625, 725
Apollo, 1017
art, 569
artifacts. *See* ritual artifacts
asceticism, 618, 620, 621, 814
Asherah, 1318
atheism, 313, 505, 615, 626
Augustine (St. Augustine, Augustine of Hip-
    po), 903, 905, 906, 907, 911, 914, 921
Australia, 549, 555, 1122

Bar Mitzvah, 1201, 1214
Bible. *See* Sections 10, 13, 15
bibliographies, 101, 102, 103, 104, 105, 338

bisexuality, 513, 1129, 1205, 1206, 2002
Bismarck, Otto von, 1040
Blake, William, 712
Blood (Blackfoot) society, 1024
Brethren, 1118
Buddhism, 1130, 1131, 1607, 1701
bull fighting, 1104, 1133
Bunyan, John, 809

Calvinism, 1335
castration, 507, 509, 561, 626, 1129, 1132,
    1145, 1203, 1211, 1336, 1407, 1418,
    1608, 2006
charisma, 625
childhood, 306, 708, 1113, 1512
Chod, 1610
Christianity. *See* Section 15
Christian Science, 1509
Christmas, 605, 610, 1141, 1513, 1515
circumcision, 1202, 1203, 1204, 1205, 1206,
    1207, 1211, 1213, 1215, 1324, 1336,
    1348, 1405
clergy, 531, 564, 603, 612
confession, 823
conversion. *See* Section 8
Confucius, 2102
creation myths, 1019, 1036, 1038, 1068,
    1069. And *see also* 'Eden, myth of'
cremation, 1325
cross-cultural research, 1914, 1917
crucifixion, 1348, 1507, 1515
Cults. *See* new religious movements (NRMs)
culture and personality, 319, 320, 1003, 1008

About the Author

BENJAMIN BEIT-HALLAHMI is Professor in the Department of Psychology at the University of Haifa. His education and teaching experience extend from Israel to the United States. He is the author of sixteen books and nearly one hundred articles and book chapters.

ISBN 0-313-27362-6

90000>

EAN

9 780313 273629

HARDCOVER BAR CODE